Breadcrumbs on My Journey

Breadcrumbs on My Journey

Celebrating Life in the City
of Brotherly Love

Richard G. Krassen
as told to David Tabatsky

Legacy Projects

To Carole

CONTENTS

Rocky, outside the Philadelphia Art Museum.
(Photo courtesy of Linda Resnick)

FOREWORD
A Word from My Editor

"SORRY, I DON'T WANT TO BOTHER YOU," Richard says to me on the phone. I picture this tall, gangly man waving an arm softly in the air, emphasizing his point about a particularly special time in his life that he wants to be sure I have not missed.

"It's got be clear that this happened in Philadelphia," he says. "Just so everybody knows it's my life story and this city has been the center of my universe since I was born. So that's important, and I just want you to know that I feel very strongly about that."

I assure Richard that this is crystal clear and a wonderful hook on which to hang his story. Every good memoir needs a home of some kind and for Richard the city of Philadelphia has always been his anchor, his challenge, and his North Star, all rolled in to one.

Putting this book together, I listened to Richard regaling the sights and sounds of this city for me, from the time he was a young boy playing outdoors in his neighborhood nearly every day of the year, rain or shine, always outdoors in the streets, enjoying himself.

Throughout this time, which began with a marathon session in Richard's home office in Center City, I witnessed Richard shift his mind and heart from speaking as a grandfather to recalling the sheer abandonment of being a young boy, with ricochets and detours through academic challenges, career strife, and huge domestic changes. Finally, he arrived at a place in his life where he can now indulge in and enjoy reflecting on the life he has lived.

It's a pleasure to watch a man explore this process, with trepidation at first, and then gradually opening up to embrace the substance of a life well-lived and celebrated, too. Richard eventually revealed interesting insights about how sharing one's story allows you to re-live experiences when you already know the outcome.

My biggest takeaway from this entire experience is that Richard Krassen really loves his family *and* the city of Philadelphia. What a great premise for sharing both of these sentiments. If only we could all feel so positive about our loved ones and our lives.

Hopefully, you will come to appreciate Richard's humor and good will, both of which he offers in abundance.

Although Richard certainly had moments of insecurity about whether he would fill enough pages to constitute an entire book, I never doubted that he would accomplish it with flying colors, as from Day One he was a willing and eager storyteller.

Richard's love of sports and music was fun to discover. I think these two pastimes and passions still make him tick today. Anyone with their own pet habits and favorite hobbies will appreciate Richard's penchant for these two activities.

But there is much more. As we all know, life unfolds according to fate and fortune, but we rarely remember it that way. In fact, we definitely do not revisit events and people—and the feelings they trigger—with any sort of pre-determined chronology in mind, or with any kind of exact outcome we can either expect or predict.

If only it were that easy.

On the contrary. Memories are fluid. They swish around, sometimes from decade to decade. And since this is Richard's story and not mine—let me step aside and let him tell it as he perceives it happened, warts and all, right down to the letter, or should I say the rebound or musical riff.

Ladies and gentlemen, may I present: Mr. Richard Krassen.

—David Tabatsky
New York City

Septuagenarian

Memories of gold,
Liver spots, wrinkles, getting old,
Searching for sunlight,
Scurrying about,
Doing it now,
Before the lights go out.

Here I am.
(Photo courtesy of Linda Resnick)

INTRODUCTION

"Here I Am."

FOR MORE THAN TWENTY YEARS, I have been thinking about writing a book about my life, but for many reasons I never did it. I thought about it. I was good at that. I began the adventure on a few occasions. I was good at that, too. The moment never seemed right, however, and I had no trouble finding excuses to postpone a genuine attempt at taking what I knew would be a huge risk.

When I met my wife-to-be in 1997, I expressed my desire to write a book during our first couple of dates. She was enamored with the prospect; in fact, her loving encouragement and support have played a significant role in my being able to reach this milestone. Several months ago, I came to a point when I was ready to jump in and move forward with this project. I don't know exactly why—perhaps turning 77 years old and knowing my time on earth is limited and I have a story to tell was the impetus. Maybe I had become fed up merely talking about it and finally needed to buckle down and actually do it.

I like to think I'm a man of action, so enough already with the procrastination! Stop talking and start writing!

Honestly, this has been a scary thing to do. I've looked at this entire process as a matter of putting myself in the most vulnerable position I could imagine, kind of like sitting in the dentist's chair for a series of Novocain shots and a root canal. While I've been willing to do that, it's come with quite a surprising result. It seems as if I have become someone I almost don't recognize: a person who has arrived at a moment in life where he is willing to take off all his clothes and stand naked in front of a packed theater of people and let them see everything about him—his man boobs, his modest pot belly, his bulbous nose, his thinning hair, and his bent ear (more on that later). And that man is me!

My birthday just passed. Many of my friends and clients are no longer with us. I have a little survivor's guilt. Why am I here? Many of them were much nicer than I am, so why me? Does God want me to continue selling life insurance? Does He want to watch me suffer, rooting for the 76ers who play no defense; rooting for the Eagles who are back to being another mediocre team after winning the Super Bowl; cheering on the Phillies as they strike out 10 times a game? Thank God I am not a hockey fan.

Maybe after I finish this book, He will pull the plug. For now, I am trying to stay in the game and play it out as completely as I can.

Go ahead. Have a look at everything good and quite possibly everything bad about me, because while I have taken great care to produce a book of quality, I have not filtered out weak spots, foibles, or shortcomings in how I portray myself. Here I am, warts and all, for better or for worse, presenting myself as an authentic human being, maybe just like you.

I decided that exploring my life was something I was finally ready to do as fully as possible—to venture forward and tell my story openly and unvarnished—naked to the bone, so to speak.

I am hoping you will share this journey with me through thick and thin, through many ups and downs, and always with my enduring love for the city and people of Philadelphia.

—Richard G. Krassen
The City of Brotherly Love

Food for Thought

The restaurant of life,
With its copious menu,
Be careful, my friend,
There is no change of venue.

Try self-fulfillment,
It's always in season.
You'll like it, I'm sure,
If it's your palate you're pleasin'.

Take a helping of understanding,
Add in friendship and caring,
And if you also choose love,
There is no charge for sharing.

PART ONE

Childhood

A Love Affair Begins

MY ROMANCE WITH PHILADELPHIA began in 1940, the year I "arrived" in our nation's birthplace. At the time, Philadelphia, with a population of approximately 1,931,000, was the third largest city in America. My neighborhood, Oxford Circle, in Northeast Philly, was definitely lively but not especially overcrowded. Up until that time, before large tracts were sold to developers preceding WWII, it had been a haven for farming.

When I was born, newly designed streets were beginning to fill up with brick and stone row houses, which still characterize this neighborhood today. During that time and for the next two decades, Oxford Circle was a white, middle-class neighborhood, and the majority of its residents were first- and second-generation Jewish Americans whose parents hailed from all over Eastern Europe. The sights and sounds and smells were decidedly Philly, specifically the area revolving around Castor Avenue.

Philadelphia is a city of American firsts—the birthplace of the United States Marine Corps, as well as America's first library, hospital, medical school, stock exchange, public park, zoo, theatre, almanac, paper mill, public school, fire department, life insurance company, bank, and business school. The "City of Brotherly Love" contains sixty-seven National Historic Landmarks and the World Heritage Site of Independence Hall. It became a member of the Organization of World Heritage Cities in 2015, as the first World Heritage City in the United States. While all of this certainly makes

2

Philadelphia a city of great distinction, what matters to me most is the fact that it is my home, in the most meaningful ways I could ever imagine.

Of course, that also includes family and friends, the Phillies, the Eagles, cheese steaks, and soft pretzels, not to mention Dairy Queen, Howdy Doody, Willie the Worm, Sally Star, Chief Half-Town, and *The Twilight Zone*.

Ladies and gentlemen, welcome to my childhood.

The Legacy of Ann

I GRADUATED FROM OUR NATION'S first business school, founded in 1881, the Wharton School at the University of Pennsylvania, in 1962. With diploma in hand, and for lack of anything better to do, I did what was necessary to earn all the licenses I needed to sell insurance. My father and grandfather preceded me in the business, so I figured it was my path to follow, as well.

I didn't become a financial success overnight. In order to initially supplement my income, I turned to substitute teaching. One of the earliest schools I taught in was Ethan Allen School, where I had attended first and second grade, and this coincidence seemed quite interesting to me at the time.

On my first day back in the school, this time as a teacher, I shared a piece of my past with the children.

"You know, when I was here, and I was only in second grade, I had a teacher named Miss Kane," I told them.

"She's still here, she's still here!" the children started yelling, excited to share the news.

At lunchtime, I made it my mission to seek out Mary Kane and speak with her. To be honest, I was a real talker in second grade, and Miss Kane found it necessary to pull me aside and put me in a chair facing the blackboard, like a timeout.

Eventually, my behavior improved; I became a better listener and more cooperative as a student, and she gave me a present of a little umbrella she had cut out of paper. I walked out of her

4

classroom twirling the umbrella, quite satisfied with myself for the positive recognition.

As Miss Kane and I started to talk, the name Karchin came up for some reason. She mentioned that she taught with a woman by the name of Karchin. She mentioned to Miss Kane that she had a daughter who had passed away at a very young age when she attended this very same school. I immediately recognized the name and told Miss Kane I knew the daughter, whose name was Ann. She and I had been classmates!

Miss Kane explained that Mrs. Karchin had become quite depressed when Ann died, and that her doctors encouraged her to have another child. Since she had poured her entire life into raising Ann and had been left devastated by her passing, having more children seemed to be a good solution. I certainly agreed with Miss Kane, and this immediately triggered my memories of Ann and our brief days together at Solis Cohen School.

Even now, approximately 70 years later, I can recall when I first noticed Ann. It was early in the school year when she went for her physical right in front of me because Karchin came just before Krassen. She smiled at me, which kind of melted my third-grade boy brain right then and there. I was convinced that I was the only boy who enjoyed that honor. I was looking forward to sitting next to her when we changed seating assignments in fourth grade. When that time arrived, I came to school every morning, anticipating talking to her and looking forward to seeing her smile again.

Days went by and she never returned to school. One day, her best friend came by and addressed our class.

"Ann is very sick, and we're all praying for her."

I prayed for Ann, too, that she would return to school, so I could see her smile again, and we could speak together.

That never came to be. Ann died of cancer, which was shocking and sad for all of us. It still haunts me today. It's hard to remember that time without thinking of the confusion and emptiness I felt, knowing someone my age could be so sick, let alone die. It made no sense to me as a boy, and still troubles me now, with grandchildren of my own.

The fragility of life is never far from my thoughts.

Years later, in my twenties, I picked up a local paper called *The Jewish Exponent,* and that week's edition featured an article on Paul Karchin, who was attending Cornell University. The last name triggered a rush of memories, and I sat down and wrote a letter to Mr. and Mrs. Karchin, who lived close by on Longshore Avenue. I told them how much I remembered their daughter and how wonderful she seemed to a young boy like me.

Mrs. Karchin wrote me back, thanking me and inviting me to her home, where I met briefly with her and her husband, a math teacher at South Philadelphia High School.

The Karchins eventually had two sons, Paul, and Louis. Louis became a prominent classical music composer and professor of music at New York University in New York City. I called him, and he kindly sent me one of his CDs. I recently discovered that Paul has a PhD in physics and works at Wayne State University.

This family saga is hard to forget. I have always valued the connection between my former teacher and the first girl I ever found special. In fact, the attraction I felt toward Ann may have been my first sense of love, as a child experiences it. Even though I never actually spoke to her, the anticipation of getting to know her was so exciting, and I spent quite some time imagining how I would sit next to her to talk and engage in a relationship.

If I could say something to Ann's parents now, I guess I would tell her parents that the tragedy of Ann's death led to the birth of her brothers and their future families, and that they would not be here if she hadn't passed away. There would be no Louis and no Paul, as well as their wives and children.

God works in mysterious ways. Mrs. Karchin never had another daughter, so there was never any possibility of comparing Ann and another little girl. God had somehow said, "I'm not going to put you through the pain of having another daughter and being forced to compare her with Ann. I'm going to give you two sons so that you will have a different experience."

My first brush with mortality left several lasting impressions.

"Dad, Are You Going to War?"

MY FIRST MOMENT OF CONSCIOUSNESS, when I actually realized I was alive in relation to a bigger world around me, occurred when I was a young boy, still standing in a crib, and heard a key clicking in the front door of our house. The sound was my father, returning from the post office where he worked at 9th Street and Market at the William Penn Annex in Philadelphia's Center City. It was Christmas time, and he was working overtime on the overnight shift. I heard him enter the house and come up the stairs.

"Dad, are you going to war?" I asked him.

He hesitated and didn't answer me right away, so like any little boy, I badgered him.

"Dad, are you going to have to go into the war?"

"I don't know," he said. "I'm not sure."

His words sounded heavy, and I must have realized, even at that very young age, that some things in life are not certain or easy to figure out. At the time, I was already conscious of the war because I played with little metal soldiers and staged make-believe wars between the soldiers. Not long after, my mother told me that the possibility of my father going into the service motivated her to make plans to rent out our house at 6749 Kindred Street in the Oxford Circle Section of Philadelphia. At one point, she even thought she'd take me all the way to Scranton, to live there with her parents.

Fortunately, the war ended before we were forced to make that move, and I was able to stay home in Philadelphia. My father never got called into the service because the military drafted single men first, before calling up any married men with children. As the war continued, they began running out of single candidates and conscripted married men, and were about to take men with children, but then the war ended, so he didn't have to go.

It's funny how I remember that fear I felt of him going to war. My parents must've spoken about it in the house, and when I overheard them, my fertile imagination went wild as a young boy. I have often thought about how my life would have been altered if we had moved to Scranton, which is a far cry from Philadelphia on many levels. If the war would have continued, my father would have most likely gone off to serve, and who knows if he would have returned or if we would have ever left Scranton?

It's interesting to see how world events can shape the life of a child and so many families. I was quite fortunate, while so many other people I know were not so lucky. The fact that my father could stay home was not to be underestimated, as it played a huge role in the childhood I continued to enjoy.

My father, whose name was Morris, was one of five children and grew up on Tenth Street in the Logan neighborhood of Philadelphia. The street was built on a slant, and some of those homes have since been torn down.

Every Sunday, like a classic American ritual, we'd take the bus and go down to my grandmother and grandfather's home for dinner, where we'd join my aunts, uncles, and cousins for a big family gathering.

My father was very smart. He graduated third in his class at Gratz High School in Philadelphia and received a full scholarship to Temple, where he majored in languages. For reasons I never fully understood, he could not get placed in a teaching job when he graduated, so he found work at a liquor store and later at the post office. Perhaps this was a result of the Depression, and my father was not the only one who suffered the fate of being forced to enter a profession he did not prefer.

Unfortunately, he worked for most of his life at a level well below his potential.

"Do you think I'm a loser?" he asked me one day when I must have been in college.

"No, not at all," I said, and I believed it.

This became a sad day for me, knowing my father could even have it in him to ask his son such a question.

I have many fond memories of my father. He often took me to the movies, just the two of us, without my mother. I remember seeing *The Monty Stratton Story* with James Stewart and June Allison, which told the story of how Monty Stratton lost his leg in a hunting accident and had to pitch in the game with one leg. For some reason, we saw *Sunset Boulevard*, with Gloria Swanson, and *Key Largo*, which I loved, with Edward G Robinson. Those days of sharing films together were very important to me.

My father also took me to my first baseball game. I was quite a Phillies fan back in 1948, when we went to see the Cardinals play my hometown favorites. The excitement and majesty of the stadium have remained with me ever since that day.

The Phillies were losing by one run in the ninth inning and had runners on first and second, with nobody out. My father may have been just as excited as I was in that moment.

"If the Phillies lose," he said, "I will buy you a Phillies cap."

Oh boy, I really wanted that cap. My father, it turns out, had a bet on the Cardinals. The next man up bunted into a triple play, and the Cardinals won. A triple play on a bunt!

"Come on, I'll get you a cap."

"I don't want the cap," I told him.

I was brokenhearted that my Phillies had lost.

From where I sit today, I would like to tell that 8-year-old boy how proud I am that he said that, knowing how much he wanted that cap but would not take it under those circumstances. If I say so myself, that kind of loyalty is rather admirable.

Years later, in 1964, my father and I watched Johnny Callison, one of my heroes, hit a home run to win the All-Star game for the National League. We shared many games together as I was growing up and even when I became an adult.

My father drove a royal marine Oldsmobile 88. What a great color! Driving around with him was so much fun for a young boy, and as I approached the age when I could drive, I looked forward to cruising the city in those wheels. One day, much to my chagrin, that beauty of a car was stolen right in front of our house and taken to a chop shop in Kensington. My father had to testify and still couldn't believe his car had been stolen.

A woman across the street by the name of Thelma Green asked him what had happened to his car.

"You tell me," he said. "You spend your days and nights watching our house. Surely you know what happened now, don't you Mrs. Green?"

Thelma had two daughters. Iris was the older, shorter, and cute one, while Cellie was tall and statuesque. Thelma got married at 16. She was very determined to have her daughters enter into a relationship as soon as possible.

Cellie once came over to our house, looking for me, while wearing a very sexy outfit. I promptly ran out the back door. My father was sure at that moment that his son was gay. I guess it never occurred to him that I was just plain scared and had no idea what to do with a girl like Cellie.

I remember another scary moment from my teenage years, when I suffered from a very bad case of acne, which made me quite self-conscious around girls and everybody else. The pimples were just awful to look at in the mirror, and thank God, they finally went away.

One day, when I was just sitting on a sofa at home, my father looked at me strangely because I had a big pimple full of pus on my neck, and he started to cry because he thought I had cancer and was dying. Fortunately, it was just another gigantic pimple, which I got rid of, reassuring him that I just had terribly oily skin, and not anything fatal like cancer. Another time, a similar thing happened, and it turned out to be a cyst, thank goodness, but for a short time it threatened to become a life-changing drama.

Maybe that was a stroke of luck—having oily skin—because now I have very few wrinkles at age 78. Of course, I have hairs in my nose and ears, and all these other interesting abnormalities that men get when they get older, including man boobs, but that's just the way it goes, I guess.

Mom in Charge

MY MOTHER, VERA, WAS THE SIXTH CHILD OF EIGHT. She was born and raised in Scranton, Pennsylvania. Her father owned a grocery store. He was a man of about five foot seven, and maybe weighed 150 pounds I used to watch when people came in to buy groceries from him. He kept a black book with each person's name inside it, along with everything they bought, so he could keep a running total. He was well organized with all of that, but the trick was getting these people to pay their bills!

He found out the payday schedule for the men who worked in the coal industry, who made up a majority of his customers. Traditionally, these guys would head straight to the bars as soon as they got paid, to kind of celebrate. My grandfather, who was rather diminutive in size, would go into those bars and address those men without any hesitation. Many of them were well over six feet tall and were not exactly skinny, either. That didn't stop him from confronting any of them.

"Mr. Murphy," he'd say, looking one of them directly in the eye, "you owe me 66 dollars and 11 cents."

Mr. Murphy and all the others would not argue. They'd fork over the money as if they knew my grandfather was not a man to mess with, which I guess he was not. That is the way he collected his due each week and made sure he got his money. I found that to be a very compelling story to hear about. I also rode on a horse and wagon with him whenever he needed to go to the wholesalers to load goods and bring them back to the store.

My mother grew up in this atmosphere, which may be why she was so neat and methodical. As far as I knew, she looked at her life as chore-driven. She woke up early each morning and got my father his breakfast at 6:30 a.m. As soon as he left the house, she would go back to sleep before making sure I was awake for school.

Quite often, especially when I was young, I was left to my own devices while she did the chores—cleaning, washing, and some cooking, too. Fending for myself meant spending a tremendous amount of time outdoors, which was fine by me.

My mother did not have a car in the early 40s and she took me along with her when she went to the Food Fair, on Castor Avenue between Unruh and Magee. I used to enjoy watching the man working inside, cutting lettuce.

We'd walk down Castor, past the Castor Bootery, where they sold shoes for the entire family. Everybody wore shoes in those days. They didn't wear sneakers, not even kids going to school. If I had gym, I would bring sneakers with me, but it seemed like wearing shoes like that to school at that time was disrespectful to teachers and the educational process. That may seem kind of crazy and silly today, but that's the way I felt at that time, and I think most children would have agreed.

The Sunray had various products for colds, hair products, and things like that. The Toddle House sold hamburgers, and Manus Drugstore, a popular pharmacy at the time, was on the corner of Unruh. Fleet's was well known for its suits and high-quality clothes for men. Fleishman's furniture store was popular, too, and all of these stores made Castor Avenue the place to be.

My mother would bring bacon fat in a jar and give it to the man behind the meat counter at Food Fair. She explained what it was for and that it contributed to the war effort. I'm still not sure what bacon fat did to help us win the war, but my mother was quite convinced of its importance at the time.

Those days with my mother were different than what I saw among my friends, perhaps because I was an only child during my early years. My mother had a ritual where she would do her chores throughout the morning, then she would take a nap every day around one o'clock for about two hours. During this time, she never let me in the house. Never. I don't know why, but she never varied from this routine. Maybe I would have bothered her otherwise and wouldn't have let her sleep. No matter what the weather was, I would spend those two hours outside. If I had to go to the bathroom, I would pee in the bushes. Fortunately, we had bushes in front of our house where no one could see me when I was that little. I would hide and pee, even when I had to stand under the trees when it rained. That's just what I did—because I had to. I didn't go over to a friend's house or look for another place, because it worked to pee in the bushes and no one ever stopped me.

Eventually, I would reconnect with my mother, when I knew she was awake and ready to have her son in the house again. That's just the way it was, and I never questioned it.

My mother was a very independent woman. She took care of her own affairs and was never needy. Being born in 1916 and growing up in the Depression meant that she spent her teenaged years struggling with her family in Scranton. It was probably tough there, and her generation grew up managing not just every penny, but every *fraction* of a penny.

The nicest thing about my mother was the fact that she gave me so much freedom. Today, many parents give their children a tremendous amount of attention, which seems wonderful at first glance, but to my mind this type of parenting can be both good and bad for the children.

When I was growing up, my mother gave me an incredible amount of latitude. She didn't ask me constantly about my school assignments, hound me about my grades, or interrogate me about how I was doing. She was simply not neurotic at all about how I was growing up or how I was doing. I was able to live my life as I saw fit, and even as a young boy this was largely up to me to determine. For better or worse, I was on my own a lot, and I think, looking back, that my parents went overboard in giving me so much freedom. I suffered later as I was growing up from a lack of structure and planning in my daily activities. I think it's essential for parents to mentor their kids in that respect, and I wish my folks had done more of that for me.

I used to threaten my mother that I would leave home. I don't know why, but I'm sure that I was mad at her for some reason. One day, she had enough of my shenanigans and took out a big suitcase, put all my clothes and possessions inside it, and before I realized what was happening, she locked me outside the front door.

The suitcase was as big as I was at that time. I stood outside on the steps, crying and banging on the front door, which she would not open no matter how hard I cried. Although I'm sure I wasn't out there terribly long, it seemed like an eternity before she let me back in, allowing me to resume life as usual with no more empty threats of leaving home.

My mother lived to be 96 years old, and when she was getting close to passing away, I brought this episode to her attention.

"Mom, do you remember when you locked me out of the house with my suitcase? I was only four-years-old."

"Yes, Richard," she said, quite sure of herself, "and you never threatened to leave home again, did you?"

Aunt Esther

I THINK EVERY JEWISH BOY who grew up in my neighborhood has a chicken soup story to tell, and I am no exception. When I was four years old, before my sister was born, my mother took me on a trolley one day along Castor Avenue to visit my Aunt Esther. We walked from home, got onboard, and were almost there when my mother realized she had left the stove on at home because she was orchestrating a slow simmer on the chicken soup she was cooking. She was worried that the house could catch fire and burn down. This caused her a ton of anxiety, and although she wasn't sure she had actually left the stove on, we both got on another trolley and went back to the house to make sure. As it turned out, she *had* left the light on, and fortunately, our house did not burn down.

We got to Aunt Esther's a little later. She was one of five brothers and sisters who grew up with my father. Aunt Edith was the oldest and played piano. I really enjoyed listening to her. Aunt Betty was a buyer for a women's clothing department. Uncle Izzy was a salesman for Krasny Products.

Aunt Esther was the youngest, and my favorite. She was a unique human being because she always wanted to give of herself and do things for other people, which I found very special, even at a young age. We went to her house on all the holidays, and she would prepare giant spreads of food, even though she did not have much money at all. I was amazed at what a generous heart she displayed. She got that from her mother, my father's mother Ida, who had the same personality.

For some reason, it always bothered me, which I mentioned to my mother, that she never had Esther to our house to reciprocate her invitations. My mother explained that Esther enjoyed hosting other people. I guess my mother was saying that she did not enjoy doing that in the same way, perhaps because she did not like putting in the effort—before and after.

I thought it would be a nice thing for my mother to do, because if someone else is constantly doing this for you then it's only fitting that you reciprocate. Who's to say what's right for everyone?

I have fond memories of Aunt Esther. She's the one who helped introduce my oldest son, Josh, to his wife, Teri, when they were both working at Einstein Hospital. Some people are always in the giving mode, and I'm lucky I had one of them in my family.

Thank You, Mrs. Ashton

MY FIRST DAY OF KINDERGARTEN remains clear in my mind. I lived at 6749 Kindred Street, and the Carnell Elementary School, the nearest one in our neighborhood, was on Devereaux Avenue, a mile and a half away. It was an easy walk except you had to cross Castor Avenue, which was a major thoroughfare with the #59 trolley going across it, which made crossing it a little dangerous, especially for a five-year-old looking at it for the first time.

My mother brought me on my first day, along with a rug, which was required for taking naps in the afternoon. At first, it was not clear to me why we needed to do that. I thought they were something mothers did and that kids didn't need them. I guess the teachers felt that five-year-old children must rest. I soon found out that we'd get tired in the afternoon and needed to lie down and take a nap. I am not sure if that is something children still do today, but I hope not, because even though I might have been tired, I always felt as if I would be missing something if I took a nap.

When my mother was ready to leave on the first day, I began crying my eyes out. I remember crying because it was the first time being in another, unfamiliar place, which proved to be quite frightening to me. So, I cried.

Mrs. Ashton was nice. She helped me feel comfortable in school. She played the piano for us, and I loved the music. We got milk every day, with cookies, too. The milk actually came from little glass milk bottles, which makes it taste good and fresh.

The problem with kindergarten was when I had to go home. Joan, a young girl in a higher grade who often took me to school, also took me home, but sometimes she would not come on time; I would get impatient waiting for her and would just walk home on my own. At five years old, that was a frightening experience, but I simply did it because there was no alternative.

The teacher didn't just let me leave and walk home! My mother paid Joan 50 cents a week to take me home safely from kindergarten. The trouble was, I got out of school before her, and I would wait for her at a certain spot until she came and walked me home. The school let me wait outside alone as a kindergarten kid!

Crazy!

This is something that would never ever happen today. I was actually outside on my own, standing under a tree, as vulnerable as can be. I guess it was a different time, when little children didn't need to be so protected. No school would let you do that now. I didn't know the difference, so it was normal for me. It wasn't horrible, except for the days I had to walk myself and try to navigate Castor Avenue. I became worried and anxious each time Joan didn't show up on time and I had to walk alone. This may be another place where the seeds of my anxiety were sown. I would come home frightened whenever I saw a police car along the way and thought they were going to arrest me because I did not wait for Joan to take me home. Maybe they would arrest me because I did something wrong. I was excited each time I went alone, and worried about it, too. What a life for a five-year-old.

A Little Hustler

I NEVER GOT AN ALLOWANCE or received money from my mom or dad to buy anything. As a young boy I had to use my creativity to figure out how to get money—legally, of course—for stuff I wanted or thought I needed. One of the ways I learned about early on was to find and collect empty soda bottles, which were made of glass at the time, and redeem them at supermarkets that sold that particular brand. It was a minor goldmine, as they would give you back five cents for large bottles and two cents for smaller ones.

I would take a shopping bag to the big empty lot at the intersection of Magee and Large, where for some reason people disposed of these bottles after they were done with them. That was a very good place to collect as many as I could fit and take them to Food Fair or Penn Fruit and get money from those stores.

I once had a bottle of Cliquot Club, which neither store would accept because it didn't come from their place. I wasn't too happy about that, so I took it into a bar on Castor Avenue to see if the bartender would take it. Three or four men sitting on bar stools thought it was really funny and laughed me right out of the bar.

I guess I was pretty fearless at the time as a young kid, but I'm still annoyed that the bartender wouldn't cash me out for the Cliquot. I mean, come on—a kid has to earn a living, too!

I also delivered *The Castor Times*, our local neighborhood paper, on a four-block route. I had to put a five-dollar deposit down for each bag of papers, and then keep trying to collect money from my customers, which wasn't always easy to do. It seems that people weren't home or had a variety of excuses, forcing me to try three or four times each to collect the cash. This became a bad business model for me, so I quit after one month. My father never interceded on my behalf, so it was a tough learning experience.

All in all, I was a pretty successful hustler as a kid. Now, even at the age of 78, although I can't redeem soda bottles or deliver newspapers, I still do similar things by negotiating for better deals. When I go to the Acme market and they mislabel an item, I take great pleasure in going to the customer service counter, where if I can prove the price is wrong I can get the item for free.

I also like that at Walgreens, on the first Tuesday of every month, they give seniors 20 percent off on sale items. I intentionally wait until the toothpaste is gone at home, so I can replace it on the first Tuesday of the month. I also love shopping at Ross on Tuesdays, which for seniors is known as "dress for less," when they offer you an additional 10 percent off if you're a senior.

I also made money as a kid by waiting outside the local Food Fair for women who had too many bags of groceries to carry and for reasons unexplained would not have a cart or a little wagon to wheel the groceries home. I was eight or nine at the time when I would approach these women just outside the store.

"You need any help carrying your groceries?"

Once in a while, someone would say yes. I would take a bag in each hand and carry the groceries to their home, usually just a few blocks away. I never had a pre-determined fee in mind and just made it up as I went along or left it up to the discretion of the woman who needed my help. It was a faulty business model, but I was a child.

Who knew? I was always happy with whatever they gave me, because it was way more than I had before. It was a nice experience. I learned to have the courage and the ability to approach people in a good way, and to ask them if they needed help. The lesson also included the ability to take rejection and to accept it when people said, "No, thank you."

This all connects to what I've done so long to make a living in my life. You can never go wrong offering your services to people. Many will say, "No, thank you," and some will start and then not work out, but just as many will get involved if you remain calm and persistent. The very act of having the courage to ask opens up the possibility to be successful. That is something I found that has served as kind of a life lesson and has been helpful over time.

Hustling to save money and make what I could was a hallmark of my youth, and that sensibility has stayed with me ever since. The attitude is something you live with, and in some ways, it becomes part of your being, which maintains its influence even later in life.

Caught on Castor

OUR NEIGHBORHOOD WAS CALLED OXFORD CIRCLE. We had three main movies houses—the Tyson, close to Tyson and Castor Avenue, the Castor, close to Unruh Street, and the Benner, next to Benner Street. Television was either non-existent or in its infant stage, so as youngsters we really enjoyed going to movies.

One Friday night, I was walking home with my friend, Fred Kauffman, from the Benner movie theatre. There were a lot of people on Castor Avenue at the time, the main thoroughfare in our neighborhood. When we reached the Sunray Drug Store, we stopped to talk with some other kids. As we were chitchatting, a few more kids gathered, and before we knew it a police paddy wagon pulled up, and the officers started taking people off the street and putting them in the vehicle. They never told us to disperse. We weren't doing anything bad; there wasn't anything broken, we weren't shouting obscenities, and weren't doing *anything* to warrant the police. Someone in an apartment above the street had taken it upon themselves to call the police because they felt there was too much noise outside.

The police hustled one kid away who was asthmatic, but they wouldn't listen to our objections. They eventually arrested 28 of us boys, jammed us all into a very small paddy wagon, and took us to the police jail on Rising Sun Avenue. We were left in one cell, all 28 of us, and the boy with asthma couldn't get his medicine. It took more than two hours before his parents were notified and they could get down there to give him his medicine. By then, all of us were getting released.

This was my first encounter with the police, and it was traumatic. I can see now how communities of color must feel about people being harassed and put into jail for no good reason. It's terrifying and highly unfair.

My father was upset. He attended the hearing with the 28 boys on the following Monday with our legal representative, Mr. Eilberg. After the testimony was completed from the policeman and everyone else, the judge said that he would keep the incident in everyone's file and expunge it at age 18. My father would not accept that, and I remember him and Mr. Eilberg arguing that this case had no business being adjudicated in a negative way, and that he didn't want any records kept of this incident.

We finally prevailed, and they did not charge us with any kind of misdemeanor, felony, or whatever you called it at that time.

That was a significant event in my life. I am certainly sympathetic, even to this day, toward people subjected to all sorts of inappropriate arrests. This is in no way an indictment of the police or police departments, who in most cases do a wonderful and honest job in this country. However, I am sure that the injustices of yesterday are still being conducted today.

Get a Life!

ONE DAY, SOME "FRIENDS" and I got into an argument with some other kids in the neighborhood. That was nothing unusual, for sure, but the way we tried to solve it certainly was, and that's just how it goes sometimes with children making their lives out on the local streets and playgrounds.

It was no different with our gang. We chose to settle things in stupid ways. In this case, we had a stone fight. We picked up stones and threw them at each other, and unfortunately, someone threw a stone and hit me smack in the head. I wound up in a doctor's office with about four or five stitches to fix a big cut on my head.

I was about seven or eight. All I would say is, don't have stone fights with people. It's not a good idea.

RICHARD G. KRASSEN

A New Member of the Family Arrives

WHEN MY MOTHER GOT PREGNANT with my future sister, she was forced to confront the fact that she had to buy me a bed, so my sister could have the crib. I will always be grateful to my sister for being born, because I might have been forced to stay in that crib until I was 18. Up until that point, even though I was getting much too tall for it, my mother seemed to think that I had no need to have a real bed until she was forced to buy one.

One Saturday afternoon, I traveled in the rain with my Aunt Sadie throughout what seemed like most of Philadelphia, running around looking for a bed and a bedroom set for me. Eventually, we got one, and I was thrilled to finally have a bed of my own, and on top of that, my own room!

As soon as I could, I set up a little pinball game of baseball, and I would spend hours each day, and at night, making up two teams hitting and fielding the ball. There was a spot for a single, double, triple, out, and whatever. Me and my new bedroom set and a baseball game. Could a boy be any happier and satisfied than that?

I vividly remember the cold January day in 1946 when my mother brought Ellen home from the hospital and she and my Uncle Abe placed her on a table.

There, for the first time, I saw my new little sister.

For reasons I can't explain, we didn't have much of a relationship. She was more than five years younger than me—and a girl—two huge factors for a boy my age. We never had any

27

conversations I can remember, and I always thought that I was pretty much an only child. For years and years, we just never talked. I don't feel good about that, but it's the truth.

Ellen had a stormy relationship with our mom as she wanted more from her than my mother would give. My mother, having grown up in a big and bustling household, always felt that she was neglected. Instead of using that experience to inspire herself to change things this time around, she took the opposite approach.

Instead of saying "I was neglected. I don't want to do that to my children," it was more like, "That's the way I was treated, so I'm going to basically do the same thing with my kids, because, hey, I felt the pain, so I'm going to let them feel the same pain, too."

Fortunately, I was born independent and enjoyed doing more things on my own. I was able to keep myself occupied and free and clear of that stress. Sadly, I didn't look out for my sister, probably because I simply didn't know any better. Ellen just wanted normal things from her mother, which should be some attention, dialogue, meaningful time, and valued experiences, which my mother didn't really understand and wasn't capable of providing.

Later, as Ellen got older, I went to her sweet 16 party at the George Washington Motor Lodge on Roosevelt Boulevard. She had a lot of cute girlfriends, but they were five years younger than me, and at that time five years was an eternity. So that was that.

Years later, when I got married, my first wife and Ellen didn't get along at all, and I maintained a limited relationship with Ellen. Only after I left my first wife did I start to develop a relationship with my sister. Now, we're pretty close. We talk at least once a week, and we're much better together. Better late than never.

Johnny, the Bread Guy

LIKE MANY FAMILIES IN OUR NEIGHBORHOOD, we had a bread man. His name was Johnny. He was a real professional who wore a uniform representing Bond Bread, the company that made a host of products we enjoyed. He came by once or twice a week, and as a young boy, this was exciting. Every once in a while, I would prevail upon my mother to buy some chocolate donuts, and she would be kind enough every now and then to get some from Johnny.

We also had a milkman from a company called Aristocrat, who sold us whole milk in glass bottles. He offered chocolate milk, but we never got any. We didn't use the other local milk supplier, who rode around with a horse and buggy and left giant mounds of horse manure on the streets, which was quite unsightly and left a very bad odor.

Harry Podel used to deliver seltzer. He would arrive in a nearby alley and bring an entire case of seltzer bottles every week. I liked seltzer back then and drank it often. We didn't get any soda, but we got seltzer, and that was fine with me.

Sweet Tooth

EVERY DAY AROUND FOUR O'CLOCK I'd come home from school and sit down in the kitchen to enjoy the snacks my mother provided—Tasty Cakes or Tasty Pies with a tall glass of milk. My favorite pies were cherry, blueberry, French apple, and lemon. I think these delicious pies cost a dime, and they were eight cents on sale. I loved the peanut butter candy cakes, too, and the cupcakes. My favorite was butterscotch Krimpets. They were the best. The jelly version was fine, but the butterscotch Krimpets? There's nothing better in this world. In fact, before I die, I would love to indulge in one last butterscotch Krimpet.

Much to my mother's chagrin, I would fill up on these snacks, so when it came time to eat dinner at 5:30 I would be not hungry. Thank goodness, because my mother was not a good cook. All her food was bland. She made liver, which I hated, because she made it with no imagination—no onions, no sauce, nothing. It was just terrible. She undercooked the vegetables, which were awful. My father wasn't big on vegetables, so we rarely ate them, which was good for me, but not especially healthy for any of us.

I will always remember those Tasty Cakes and Tasty Pies!

A New Challenge

I ONCE HAD THE IDEA to walk from northeast Philadelphia to the state of New Jersey. This was in July, when the temperature was probably in the 90s, and it was usually quite humid, too. I convinced my two friends, Ted and Richard, to accompany me on my great idea—to cross the Tacony Palmyra Bridge, about two or three miles from our home, and leave the comforts of home in Pennsylvania for the unknown wilds of New Jersey.

I filled a canteen with grape juice in case we got thirsty, not realizing that grape juice would quickly sour in the heat, leaving us with nothing else to drink.

It was a long, hot walk, especially the return trip, and we didn't even encounter anything exciting in New Jersey. The next day, Richard's mother came to my mother, quite unhappy and upset.

"Your son made my son sick," she said. "Now, he has the flu, and he's dehydrated. I had to take him to the doctor, and I blame your son for talking my son into walking to New Jersey."

You may be wondering why I wanted to walk to New Jersey. It was simply something to do. I thought going to a completely different state would be new and fun, something different, but it turned out to be not much more than hot and sweaty.

Yellow Slickers

MY PARENTS' MAIN SUMMER VACATION destination was the shore in Beach Haven or some other place by the water, depending on how many days they had free. One of our rare vacations outside the area took us to Niagara Falls. What I remember most is when we put on these big yellow slickers and stood underneath the falls, where the water came speeding down on top of us all.

Getting drenched like that was quite exciting. We also took a boat ride at the base of the falls, and I lost a sneaker along the way. I don't know how it happened. My foot was resting on a ledge, and before I knew what happened, my shoe fell into the water. In spite of that, we had a good time, and it shows how just a few days together can create a nice family memory.

Can't Save My Tonsils

I USED TO GET EARACHES every time I got a cold, which were very painful. My mother treated them with a medicine called Auralgon, which she heated in a blue bottle. For the most part, this worked, but it was debilitating each time it happened.

When I was seven or eight, I had to have my tonsils out for what I thought at the time was no good reason. It seemed like every kid I knew in our neighborhood had them out, and for unspecific reasons. The doctors told us all that tonsils were not necessary. If you ask me, I think those guys had quite a hustle going on.

Anyway, I went to the hospital on Greene Street early one morning, where I was given a gown and a bed and told to lie down and wait. A very tall, muscular African-American male came by, threw me over his shoulder like a sack of potatoes, and took me to the operating room, where a sheet was put over my head.

That was scary. I woke up with my mother next to me and I ate ice cream. I guess it wasn't as bad as it seemed.

In Living Black & White

IN 1947 OR 1948, my father bought our first television set, a ten-inch RCA Victor. My Uncle Harry worked at RCA, and a year earlier he had built a seven-inch TV all by himself. We became the only people on our block of Kindred Street to own a TV. Every Friday afternoon, a special show of cowboy movies and cartoons would come on, and we invited all seven or eight children on the block to come into our house and share the fun of watching them on TV. They'd show *The Range Busters* and *Hopalong Cassidy*.

They used to ask Hopalong, "What do you want to drink?" and he would always say, "Sarsaparilla." Buck Jones drank buttermilk. A fight would invariably ensue, with Hoppy or Buck always winning.

I loved those cowboy movies, which they showed a lot back in those days. In the fifties, they had movies like that on all the time. Some of my favorites were Roy Rogers, Gene Autry, Bob Steele, and The Range Busters. It was a wonderful time.

Having a TV was fantastic, even when I watched by myself. I saw the 1948 Philadelphia Eagles championship win against the Chicago Cardinals. They beat them seven-nothing in the snow. There had been a huge snowfall the night before the game, and they were still digging out when the game started. Steve van Buren, who was a great runner for our team, carried the ball almost every time. I was alone watching our ten-inch, black and white TV with great joy, as the Eagles won that game and the championship. For a kid like me, it was very exciting.

They used to show college basketball games on TV, too, which I really enjoyed, but my favorite TV shows included *Your Show of Shows* with Sid Caesar, *I Love Lucy*, *The Jackie Gleason Show*, *The Red Skelton Show*, *Frontier Playhouse*, *Amos and Andy*, *Playhouse 90*, *Racquet Squad*, and *Leave it to Beaver*.

My True Love

TELEVISION WAS DEFINITELY A COOL INVENTION, but my true love was always radio. I could lie in my bed for hours at night, listening to one show after another, including *Gangbusters*, *Luck's Theater*, *The Lone Ranger*, and *The Fat Man*, who used to walk down the street and get on a scale. Radio was great, and still is.

The person I loved the most on the radio was a man by the name of Jean Shepherd. He was what you would call a monologist. He would just talk by creating things out of thin air and talking about them for hours—little minute things that fascinated me. When he lived in Indiana, he would talk about meeting someone and the conversations they would have.

For some reason, he really captured my interest. People would come up to him and say, "Jean, how do you do that? How do you recall those moments? How do you make it so interesting?" He said, "Anybody has the ability to do this. Anybody who wants to take the time can do the same thing." Of course, this was not true.

I loved the radio. I'd listen to a show called *The Long John's Show*, which would sometimes last until nearly three in the morning. I would get two, maybe three hours of sleep before I would have to get up and get ready to go to school, but I didn't care, because those were really, really good times.

The big event arrived when my parents gave me my own Zenith radio. Actually, they didn't really *give* it to me. My father had initially bought it for my mother for her birthday. I was never demanding with my parents, but for some reason I took the Zenith and made it my own and my mother never said a word.

I loved that radio and listened to it for hours. I would tune in to jazz stations and started to love it so much I couldn't go to sleep without it. I liked the African-American stations, with Georgie Woods and Philadelphia's own legendary icon, Jocko Henderson, because both of them played doo-wop and rock and roll. I developed a wonderful love of music from listening to the radio.

I spent a lot of time alone, which I remember to this day being a very lonely existence, so thank God I had the radio. It's different today, because parents engage with their children and share their time together. There was much more isolation back when I was growing up between parents and children—for me and probably many other children of my generation.

My parents had their own interests. My father worked long hours, and my mother was always busy doing family chores. My sister was much younger and was always asleep before me. So, this left me alone to indulge in the joys of radio, the one thing I loved more than anything else. I would sit in my room in the afternoons after school and during the evenings and escape into the world of radio. All during the forties, before television was even commercially available, I would listen to the radio, to shows like *The Fat Man* and *The Gangbusters*, with detective Johnny Diamond.

One day, when I was eight or nine, for reasons I still can't fully explain, I used my penknife to carve my name into the side of the radio. Maybe I needed some recognition of my existence, or something like that, because I carved "Richard Garry Krassen" into the side of my radio. When my mother saw it, she went ballistic for two reasons: one, about me carving my name into the radio, and second because I misspelled "Gary," which only has one "r."

I kept the radio and continued listening happily to Sid Mark on Friday nights, when he played "Friday with Frank," featuring Frank Sinatra. I would listen to Georgie Woods, "The Man with the Goods," play black doo-wop music, which I loved.

Back then, black music and white music did not mix. Many white advertisers wanted to keep white performers singing songs separate from black performers and what they chose to sing. We had stations in Philadelphia, like WCBG with Joe Niagara, the Rockin' Robin, who played white music, and people like Pat Boone covered black artists, such as Little Richard, singing Tutti Frutti, trying to make them popular on white radio. I listen to doo-wop every morning. Jerry Blavet, a local icon here in Philly, probably knows more about doo-wop than any living person.

As I got older, I listened even more to Jean Shepherd, as I was interested in what he had to say about meeting girls and talking to them. I was captivated by all of his discourse.

I listened at night to Philadelphia Warriors basketball games, in the forties, and to countless games of the Phillies and the Eagles.

Doo-wop was what I loved the most, and still do. I would wait for these songs to come on and then just lie back and soak it in or dance by myself in my room.

My Top Ten +1 faves go like this:

"The Story Untold," by The Nutmegs.

"You Cheated, You Lied," by The Shields.

"Pretty Little Girl," by The Monarchs.

"In the Still of the Night," by the Five Satins.

"Teardrops," by Lee Andrews and the Hearts.

"Earth Angel," by The Penguins.

"My True Story," by The Jive Five.

"One Summer Night," by The Danleers.

"Whispering Bells," by the Del-Vikings.

"Image of a Girl," by The Safaris.

"Book of Love," by The Monotones.

My First Poem

TOWARD THE END OF THE FIRST SEMESTER of fourth grade, we had a little talent show in our class at Christmas time. Kids would sing or play the harmonica or do whatever it is kids did back then to amuse each other.

I took a decidedly different approach that year. I had a poem to read, written by my mother and me. My classmate, Fred Braun, introduced me.

"Next, here is a poem by Richard."

I whispered to him that my mother helped me write it, so he added "and his mother," and all the kids laughed. I don't know why, but I felt that since my mother helped me write it, she should get credit for helping me. Everybody found it amusing. I was just trying to not take full credit for something I didn't do by myself.

I think it's important to give everyone credit when you do anything. Later on, when I played basketball or did other group activities, I always tried to remember that life is a team game. We are all just members of different kinds of teams. We're not individuals only. It takes other people to help us achieve things and do what's great. That should never be forgotten. It should always be acknowledged.

Who Knew?

WHEN I WAS TEN OR ELEVEN, my synagogue, Temple Shalom, sponsored a Cub Scout pack. Every Friday afternoon, we went to a den mother's house, where a lovely woman would host us for arts and crafts and different projects for an hour and a half after school.

One of the most interesting things we did in those days was put on a minstrel show. This revolved around the presence of what was called an Interlocutor, someone who would sit on a stool, such as a character like Uncle Remus, who would call on kids, made up in blackface to tell him jokes. My father gave me a joke to ask him:

"Why did my nose get to school before I did?"

"I don't know," the Interlocutor would say. "Tell me."

"Because my nose was running," I'd say, "and I was walking."

Everybody laughed, and one by one, as each child told a joke with the Interlocutor, the audience roared or groaned.

Then, still in blackface, we sang a spiritual song, or something like "Swanee" or "Old Kentucky Home" or whatever else was popular in those days.

I never gave a thought to the fact that I was doing something degrading by wearing blackface and acting foolish. Now, of course, I know that's not right, but as a child, I didn't know any better; it seemed okay, and my parents never said a word. Who knew?

Surviving in Scranton

WE USED TO DRIVE TO SCRANTON three or four times a year to visit my mother's family. There was no northeast extension, so we'd pass through every small town on the three-and-a-half-hour ride. My sister Ellen and I relieved the boredom by guessing who had the most cows on their side of the road. Unfortunately, after one or two trips, we knew which side had the most cows, so that game became predictable. On top of that, Ellen invariably became carsick, because the ride was not particularly pleasant.

My parents stayed in the house most of the time, which left me to my own devices outside, where I would run up and down the nearby slate mines. I took a bat and clothespins and made up a game where I would throw a clothespin up in the air and hit it, and designated certain places as a single, double, triple, home run, or an out. I created games with two teams, which is how I passed my time in Scranton while my parents and sister were visiting in the house.

Those were days you had to be creative in order to survive. There was no TV or cell phones, and no parents engaging you, at least not mine, in reading or games. With them, it was more like, "Hey, we're busy, son, so find something to do."

I don't think my folks were bad parents. It was simply a different era, and that's just the way it was.

One time, on the drive home, we passed through the city of Easton, where we stopped for lunch. The people there were trying to find candidates to adopt three or four cute little puppies who had been rescued from a recent flood. I had never had a dog, and as we drove away, I kept begging my father to get one. Finally, I guess he got tired of me nudging him, so he turned the car around and we went back.

I named the dog Mickey. We knew nothing about taking care of a dog, and my parents weren't any help in that regard, so it didn't take long before the whole thing became an unfortunate mess. Mickey peed all over the basement floor, where we put down newspapers. I never walked him, and neither did my parents. Finally, we put him in the back yard where we had a fence, but he squeezed between the bars and got out and kicked over a couple of our neighbor's milk bottles. He laughed, and smiled at us, because he thought it was pretty funny. It wasn't funny to my mother, though; she called the SPCA, and Mickey was taken away.

That was the end of my history with dogs. I never had one again, but I've had many cats, which are much more to my liking. I live in an apartment house that is dog-friendly and see tons of dogs, and they're all fine, but I have no desire to take care of them, I just enjoy seeing them.

I am considering finding someone who would make me an artificial dog out of wood or some other material, so I could carry it into the elevator and out of the door to make people think I'm sympathetic to dogs without actually having one.

A year or so later, I got two turtles, Wadley and Gadley. One night, we heard some noise in the house, and as we went downstairs, my mother or I stepped on poor Wadley, and he was crushed. I was sad for quite some time, but Gadley lived a while longer. Maybe I should get another turtle instead of a wooden dog.

A Different Side of My Dad

MY FATHER LIVED WITH A LOT OF PAIN, which he didn't want to share with me. Unfortunately, he was quite a fragile human being and was hospitalized with a nervous breakdown when I was ten years old. My mother had me stay for a week with my Aunt Edith, my father's sister, who lived on Hutchinson Street in the Logan section of Philadelphia, across from the Bernie playground. My cousin, Stanford, lived there, too.

I visited my father at the hospital with my mother and sister, but since we were too young to go inside, we had to meet our father at the entrance gate, where we were forced to talk to him there, as if he were a prisoner who couldn't be let out into the free world. It was a very trying time, especially when he started to break down in tears right before they had to put him in the hospital. I realized then how awful it would have been if he had been forced to go into the service when I was younger. Fortunately, he was able to continue his life without that experience, but I wondered at that time how bad it might have been.

I saw no previous indication at home of anything like a breakdown. My father just started crying out of the blue. Whatever had been developing inside him, he had kept in check or hidden, and we never talked about it. He was in the hospital for a week or two, then he came home, and was pretty level after that. He eventually went back to teaching, which is what he really wanted to do. He taught languages at Fels Junior High in Philadelphia.

During the week my father was in the hospital, I stayed with my cousin's family. One day, Stanford and I were across the street in the Bernie playground, when out of nowhere, a gentleman showed up who turned out to be Willie Puddinhead Jones, the starting third baseman for the Philadelphia Phillies. This baseball team was called the Wiz Kids in 1950 and won the National League pennant. He was renting a room in a nearby house, because at that time baseball players made very little money. In fact, most of the time they had to work part-time jobs to make a suitable living.

Willie came outside to see the neighborhood kids for what seemed like hours. He spoke about how he had grown up, what he did in school, and how he became a baseball player. I'll never forget his kindness and his connection with all of us kids, talking about baseball and life. It was a meaningful experience for all of us, and for one day at least, it surely took my mind off my father's troubles.

Today, of course, it is a whole different game. Major league baseball players make a lot of money, and none of us regular people ever see them up close or have a chance to talk to them. Back then, when I was ten years old in 1950, baseball was king, and everyone loved it. Willie Jones was a wonderful third baseman and had a glove that looked like a rag. He hit with power and had a good average.

More important, it was so heartwarming to meet up like a regular guy who chose to spend his time with us kids and talked to each of us like we were just people, not children, talking about regular things. It was one of the nicest afternoons I had as a child.

Stone-faced

MY FATHER LOVED THE GAME OF PINOCHLE. He had people at our house every Wednesday night. They didn't rotate. They didn't go to other people's houses, probably because the wives didn't want those men in their house, but my father prevailed, and we had our pinochle game in our house.

I was eleven and allowed to watch if I said nothing. Zero. No facial expression. Nothing! I had to be stone-faced and not say a single word. That was the rule. Break the rule, no more watching pinochle. The guys played partners, as opposed to firehouse, which I believe was a game with three people. Partners is played with one partner, and whoever gets the most points wins, plus whatever bonuses are accrued. They rotate partners, so you play a game or two with one partner and then you get a different one.

Al smoked cigars, the worst smelling cigars in the history of mankind. You could not get the stink of his cigars out of the house for like a week. You could open the windows and spray stuff all over the place, but nothing mattered. Nobody said not to smoke cigars, so Al did. I was sick every day walking through the dining room where he left his cigar smoke.

One time, I was watching my father play cards when for some reason, I looked behind a man named Nate, who got dealt a flush, with an ace, king, queen, jack and a ten. That was worth fifteen points, which was a lot. He was looking at the cards, and I was looking at the cards, and I knew he had a flush, and I'm maybe eleven or twelve years old, and he doesn't bid. What? I couldn't believe it. I still remember what happened after his turn passed, when he put his hands on his head and said, "Oh, my God!" I still remember watching that and seeing him miss his chance.

My father won sometimes, but he also lost seven dollars at a time, or nine or ten bucks, which was not an insignificant amount of money back in those days. I used to think about things like that and wonder how that worked.

Al won $24 one night, which was like winning the lottery, as it represented maybe a week's worth of work in one shot.

My cousin, Bruce, played pinochle in Scranton with my Uncle Harry, my uncle Max, my mother's father, and my father. Bruce was a kibitzer. He had to talk, no matter what. He used to kibitz with his father when he got his hand, which made my father furious.

"I don't want Bruce here unless he shuts his mouth," my father used to say to us when we were away from the house, but Bruce never did stop talking. I kept quiet, even when he was irritating me, too. I know that many things upset my father, and I always felt that if that was the case you had to tell people. You have to let people know if you're unhappy with something. My father would not let me talk, however, and there was no reason for my uncle Max, God bless his soul, not to tell my cousin.

Bruce became successful in Florida and was ordained as a rabbi. In fact, he came to Philadelphia and married me to my second wife, Carole, in 2004. All is forgiven with Bruce, for talking during those pinochle games with my father.

Golden Words

I VIVIDLY REMEMBER LISTENING TO BASKETBALL games in my room before I ever played one. Philadelphia Warrior basketball was broadcast live in the 1940s. Matt Goukis, Sr. announced the games, and I listened to them all, beginning when I was about eight years old. That's the same time my father took me to his friend's house. Irv Brodie worked in the physical education department at Overbrook High School, and he offered me an old basketball.

"Here Rich, this ball we don't use anymore. You can have it."

Golden words.

I walked over to the playground every day and shot baskets in the shadow of Spruance Elementary School, which was nearest to our house. They had little circular baskets with no nets, just a small metal circle. I played with friends, even when it was freezing cold and snowing. That didn't bug any of us. We'd just bring some shovels and dig our way to a relatively smooth surface, and nobody thought anything of it as long as we were playing ball.

There were very few days of the year when I wasn't playing outside. In those days, everybody was outside, and all of us boys played different games and switched it up, too.

At Spruance, as a twelve-year-old, I played in my first basketball league, which consisted of four teams. Ours was called the Hot Shots. We wound up in third place and still made the playoffs. The first team played the fourth, and the second played the third. We narrowly beat the second-place team and wound up playing the team in first place. They beat us handily in the regular season and had excellent shooters, so we decided to press them full court for the entire game. Luckily, we had a couple of guys who were tenacious defenders and we wound up beating the regular season champs in four straight games.

They gave out trophies at the ceremony after we won the championship. I treasured the little trophy, which probably didn't even cost a dollar to produce. They said it would be engraved as "The Hot Shot Champions," but that never happened.

I put that little trophy on my mantle in our new house on Large Street, and every day I came home, no matter how I felt, when I saw that trophy on the mantelpiece, I felt happy.

One day, I came home from school and the trophy was gone.

"Mom, what happened to the trophy?"

I was in a panic.

"They came and asked for it back," she said.

"What do you mean?"

She explained to me that they had told her it wasn't mine to keep, that I had to win the championship three years in a row in order to do that. I had some big questions bouncing around in my head as soon as I heard that. First, this was a brand-new teen league, so how could anyone have previously been on a team for three years? Second, why would they want a trophy back that probably wasn't even worth a dollar? Third, and this was the most important question: Why did my mother give it back to them? Why didn't she say, "No, I'm sorry, but you're not getting this trophy back because my son earned it."

Losing that trophy was hugely disappointing, but I got over it. What an absurd decision! They wanted to reuse it for the next league and decided they would save on a dollar wherever they could. Fair enough, as times were tight, but I don't know how I can excuse my mother for not fighting for me.

Imagine somebody knocking on your door. You're a kid and you have a favorite toy, and these men knock at your door and ask your mother to give her son's favorite possession (beside his radio) back to them. "Sorry, but we need it back right now." And then your mother gives it to them without a fight.

I was more upset with my mother than the cheapo guys running the league. It was the first trophy I had ever won in my life. Why would she give it away? It wasn't the actual trophy and its material value; it was what it represented. You had to win four out of seven games to earn it; that was a huge accomplishment for us and a very big deal to me. We were 12 years old and won a best of seven series like they do in the NBA. On top of that, we won four in a row! Against a team we were supposed to lose to! I got this little freaking trophy to take home and put on my mantelpiece, and then they came, and my mother gave it back!

Mom! What were you thinking?

It was like the basketball mafia came into our home and invaded our privacy.

"We're here from the Spruance school where your son played basketball, I know he won the championship by winning four straight games against a team we all thought was unbeatable, but that trophy was not meant to be kept, and he only gets it if he wins the championship three years in a row."

My mother just agrees and gives him the trophy, just like that.

Why the fuck would she give him the trophy? I mean, come on! Some things are hard to let go of, no matter how long ago, and this is definitely one of them.

The One I Dropped

DURING FIFTH GRADE at Spruance Elementary School, Mr. Catalano assembled a softball team. I was the only fifth grader on a team of sixth graders, but during one game against Carnell, he put me in center field. I barely had my bearings when a line drive came right at me. I was in perfect position to catch the ball, but for some reason it hit the heel of my glove and bounced out of my grasp. I bent down to pick it up and inadvertently kicked it, forcing me to run around the outfield, trying to pick it up. Sadly, the batter from Carnell ended up with an inside-the-park home run.

That was a painful experience, and we all beat ourselves up about things we do poorly. I was no exception. I wanted to do everything right, especially on the playing field. That was a tough moment, and unfortunately, I must recognize that I still carry it with me.

Fortunately, I got to start in left field the following year as a sixth grader, and we beat Carnell ten to nine. I caught a couple of fly balls hit to me, and that pretty much redeemed my big mistake from the year before, but it's still hard to forget the one I dropped.

We all have moments in our lives when we mess up or do poorly and feel a little upset. We also have done many good things. However, for some reason, things we have messed up or failed at stay with us longer and dig deeper than things we have done well. This is a condition that affects most human beings. Happiness and feeling good from our achievements never impacts us as much as our failures.

Hopefully, we learn from them.

For example, one day when I was playing hardball with my friends on a lot on Magee Avenue I wound up catching without a mask, which was kind of stupid now that I think about it. Someone had to catch the ball when the pitcher threw it.

Somebody foul-tipped the ball, and it came flying back and hit me flush in the eye. I cried and wouldn't let go of holding my face. By the time I got home, my eye was swollen shut, and I couldn't see out of it for a week. The whole thing was quite traumatic. I advise anyone playing catcher behind the plate to make sure you wear a mask. It's important.

Brain Freeze and Valuable Lessons

BY THE TIME I REACHED SIXTH GRADE, I was one of the tallest boys in my class. A young girl named Ruth Fine wrote a play, and she wanted me to be Roger Williams, the guy from colonial Rhode Island. I was taller than her, and she played Mrs. Williams. I worked on the lines and prepared for the play we presented in front of our class. I kind of knew my lines when we rehearsed, especially the day before when I went over all of them with my mother.

The next day, I froze up midway through the play, and just couldn't remember anything. I forgot all of my lines. Ruth knew every part, and she said them under her breath, which enabled me to continue. It was the last play I was ever in. Being an actor was not my calling. Ruth had a beautiful smile and lovely dark eyes. I had a crush on her. She went on to become a major force in the art world.

Since drama was not my thing, I was happy to be in math class, and I was fond of my teacher, Morris Kauffman, who was the uncle of my future best friend, Fred Kauffman. During lunchtime, he would put his feet up on his desk and smoke a pipe.

Right before lunch each day, Morris would go through mathematical exercises. He would give out numbers for multiplication problems at breakneck speed. After maybe a minute or two, he would say to the class, "If you know the answer, go to the board and write it down."

I almost always had the answer, but I'd keep it to myself. One day, three of my classmates went up to the board and all of them

52

had it wrong. I did not go up, even though I had the right answer. I was reluctant because I was afraid I might be wrong. That was one of the best lessons I've ever learned in my life.

Number one, you have to believe in yourself. Number two, you can't be afraid to fail. Real failure is not trying. In my life, and in my teachings to my three boys and grandchildren, I always advocate for them to go after whatever they want and to not be afraid of failing or not getting things just right. The worst mistake you can make is failing to act and regretting that choice later.

During sixth grade, the boys and girls in my class had parties on the weekends, where they would play post office and different games that included kissing. When a girl asked me to go to one of those parties, I told her I had to check with my mother.

I never went to that party and was never invited to another. I regretted not being there, and still don't know why I told that girl I had to ask my mother, especially when it involved kissing, which is definitely *not* something you ask your mother about. I guess I was scared to go, and sadly, I never got to play post office.

That was another lesson about fear of failure and the inhibition that can keep you from trying new things. Some of that is normal. I wonder if my father's fragile state had some influence on me being so self-protective. I think my mother was protective of herself, more than my father. My mother liked everything to be clean and neat. She would get her paper in the morning, and by three or four o'clock in the afternoon it was already thrown away. She hated clutter. She liked things orderly and predictable. She didn't like anything to throw her off. Maybe that didn't give me the feeling of being open to taking new chances. In any case, I still wonder what it must have been like to play spin-the-bottle on the weekends.

Short and Sweet

DURING ELEMENTARY SCHOOL, we participated in the Frankford Relays. I was chosen to start off the 440-yard race and was followed by my teammates, Donny Fruchman, Lanny Forman, Bill Richman, and Jeffrey Hughes. Handing off the baton was critical in order for us to be a successful team. I was certainly one of the fastest at the time, if not the fastest, and we won by almost 20 yards. That was a thrilling encounter.

RICHARD G. KRASSEN

Sleepaway Camps

I WAS ELEVEN OR TWELVE YEARS OLD when I went to my first overnight camp, an inexpensive week with the Boy Scouts in spartan accommodations, which is probably a generous description. The beds were so bad you could barely get a good night's sleep. The food appeared to be the same for each meal, only with a different name, as if we would not notice.

Lester Goren, one of my friends, fell into a cesspool one day, and word got around camp pretty fast that poor Lester had fallen into a real stinkpot. They had to hose him down. That was the last time I actually saw Lester; I hope he's okay and that the smell has passed out of his system by now.

We did a lot of okay things at that camp, but the incident with Lester was probably our biggest highlight of that week.

The following summer, I went to Wyomissing camp for two weeks, which I liked. Local brought kids in from all over the city. I did a stupid thing to my counselor, Ted Wexler, which I regretted right away, when I took his shoelaces and shoes and tied knots in all the laces. Why I did that, I have no idea, but I would apologize to him now if he were alive.

We had wonderful baseball games there, which were especially good because we played hardball instead of softball, which was the norm at most camps. I pitched one game and went the entire nine innings on a 90-degree day when my parents were there. We lost 20

55

to 11 because our team made at least ten errors, allowing lots of unnecessary runs to score.

That camp also had contests of football throws, and I could throw one pretty far. In fact, my throw went way farther than anyone else's, which was really nice that first year.

The second year, we played basketball. We had a game against a fellow named Jim McNickel, who played for West Catholic and stood about six foot six. I was able to keep him away from the basket, and we beat them.

We were sure we'd win the championship. We took the court against a much smaller team, but their counselor (each team was allowed to play one staff member) was this fellow named Joey Goldenberg, who had played at West Philly High against Wilt Chamberlain. To make a long story short, he never missed a shot and we lost by 15 points, which was quite shocking.

One time, while playing in a volleyball game with a man named Jack Snapper Devine, who played basketball at Villanova, he screamed at me because I didn't dive for a ball. I still wake up and hear him screaming: "Krassen, dive for that ball!" He was an incredible competitor. I really enjoyed my two stints at Wyomissing and the characters I met there. For example, Jack Lopinsan was our team's shortstop at camp. He was later convicted for having his wife and business partner killed. Ouch!

I went to an overnight camp called Kittatinny, which was a lot of fun. My friend, Fred Kauffman and his family owned the camp. That's where I met a good friend of mine, Dr. Myron Rodos, who is a practicing physician in North Philadelphia.

We had a color war, including a rough game of touch football. We lost that game due to too many fumbles, but our team won the color war, which gave us bragging rights for the rest of our stay.

In the summer of 1955, the man in charge of managing the camp was Chuck Smerns.

One day, he approached me to ask if I would consider doing something for him. His niece, Sonia, who was attending camp with me, was not happy and wanted to go home. We were supposed to go by bus to a playhouse that evening, and he asked me if I would ride with her up and back. She was attractive—tall and slim and blond—and kind of shy. I had no one else I was planning to sit with, so I agreed. We went to the show and sat together, as if we were on a date. We didn't say much on the way to the show or during the performance, but on the way home the conversation became a little more fluid until we got back to camp.

The next afternoon, as my friends and I were walking back to our bunk from an activity, we passed by Sonia's cabin.

"Where's Sonia?" I asked one of the girls.

"She went home this morning."

I guess my conversation skills weren't too convincing.

Summer camp is where I hit my longest ball in softball, over 320 feet. I only got a triple, because the boy in left field was really fast and his throw held me at third base.

All of the camps I attended were special because they often produced lasting relationships, some of which I still cherish today.

Street Ball

WHAT STICKS WITH ME MOST about growing up in northeast Philadelphia were the street games we played as children. Anything with a ball would do just fine—box ball, hoseball, wireball, or stickball—as long as it involved a ball-like object, we played it—alone, with a friend, or in keen competition with teams.

When my father came home from work, he would always stop to get me Charms or Lifesavers or some little treat, which was nice. My favorite moments were when he played catch with me for 20 minutes before he went inside the house. When he whistled for me at 5:30 p.m., no matter what I was playing, I would drop everything and head inside for dinner, because I knew that this time was sacred.

That's when he and my mother wanted to eat, and I couldn't say, "I need another inning" or "I need another 10 minutes."

There was no discussion.

Our street had sewers, which was a real problem because balls cost money, and nobody had much to spare. Frannie Fernback used to hold his brother, Joey, by the legs while he reached down into the sewer to retrieve lost balls.

From an early age, my life was filled with all kinds of wonderful games on the street, and since they all involved a ball, or something at least resembling one, that's how the games got their name, too.

For example, wireball was a great game, which I played often against Joe Silver, who later tried out for professional baseball. There were electrical wires hanging between most of our houses. They were all over the place, just like trolley tracks. If you hit the wire and the other kid didn't catch it, it'd be a run and you'd score. If you hit two wires, it would be a double. If you threw it up and they missed it, you'd get a single, but if you hit three different wires, it would be a triple.

Joe had a tremendous arm and would throw the ball up about a thousand feet in the air (or so it seemed), expecting me to drop the ball. His goal was never to hit the wires; it was just to throw the ball so high that I'd get dizzy before it came down, so I'd drop the ball. For some reason, as high as he would throw it, whatever spin he would try, I would catch the ball. However, I was able to hit the wires because my concentration was good for that; he was unhappy about it and wasn't a particularly good sport. It was something I cherished, to be able to beat the great Joe Silver at wireball.

With wallball, you hit a wall with a ball, and somebody's got to catch it in order to get three outs. If you hit it so hard that it goes over your head, you get a home run; if it goes in front of you, you get a single, and it goes on from there.

I could talk stickball all day long in great detail. It was probably the most prominent game we played as young kids growing up. We would put a large block on a brick wall in the schoolyard, which would serve as the strike zone. We'd use a tennis ball, if we had one, or what was called a pinky or a pimple ball. One person would pitch, and the other person would hit the ball; depending on where you hit it, you'd get a single, double, triple, or home run.

Fred Kauffman and I played stickball every day. I pretended to be one major league team, and he would be another. We would've played well past 5:30 each day if we hadn't been called home to dinner.

My friend, Mel, and I played against another friend, Tom Carey, and his brother, Frank. Tom was the starting shortstop for the Lincoln High School city championship team in 1957 (Lincoln's first major sport city title) and the Public League Championship in 1958. Frank earned his Ph.D. in Organic Chemistry and is currently a

Professor Emeritus at the University of Virginia. His chemistry textbooks are used worldwide.

I will never forget one game in particular when we were teenagers. It was getting dark, and Tom and Frank were winning 16-13 in a game we were playing on the field at Fels Junior High School in northeast Philadelphia. We could hardly see the ball. I was up with three men on and two outs, and Frank was throwing really hard. For some reason, which none of us can explain to this day, Frank decided to throw me a changeup; I hit it over the fence, and we won 17-16. Tom still laments that loss today when we talk about it, which we still do! We have decided that Frank chose to have some fun and throw a changeup instead of his fastball, which I crushed. That was a great game.

Boxball was another wonderful game. It was somewhat scientific, with a third baseman, second baseman, shortstop, first baseman, pitcher and catcher. You had to get the person who pitched to throw you a low pitch, because you wanted to punch it through the infield in order to get a single, double, triple, or home run. If you hit it in the air out of the infield, it was an out. You had to hit the ball on the ground. When you got the pitch you wanted, you had to use your hand, many times an open hand, and sometimes you made a fist, and figured out a spot where you could place the ball so the fielders couldn't catch it. It was a very scientific game, and I loved it.

Some people played halfball, where we'd cut a ball in half and use it for the same kind of games. This was done to preserve the balls we had, because sometimes they got pretty scarce.

Hoseball was different. We took an old hose and used a knife to cut it in little pieces. We'd take a bat and people would throw the piece of hose and you hit it, just as if it was a real ball. That was hoseball.

We also used local hoses to drink water, because none of us would dare run into our houses when we were thirsty and disturb anyone, when we were supposed to be outside playing.

Each game had its own graduating levels of skill. All of them were different and presented their own challenges. This was the nicest thing, as it created a way to connect with other children in the neighborhood; you'd need to come together to play any of these games, and cooperation and compromise were the keys to keeping the games going. Everybody would play, and no one was ever excluded.

We used all kinds of balls to play these games. A pimple ball, which people might remember, is usually a white ball with little pimples on it. The liveliest ball was called a pinky, which we usually used for stepball. Everybody had steps in front of their house, and you tried to hit it into the cracks, so when you hit the step at the base of the crack the ball would go the farthest; that's how you kept score.

We always had a person monitoring traffic. We would stop for the cars and the occasional old man or lady who was extra slow crossing the street. Every city had kids playing street games, I'm sure, but Philadelphia was a non-stop scene of flying balls and screaming boys, having the time of their young lives.

My favorite game at school was dodgeball, especially when we used two balls. Everyone got hit. It became a metaphor for life, I guess, because with many balls in the air, eventually we all get hit. Nothing beat the camaraderie and endless excitement of playing ballgames outside in our neighborhood each and every day, rain or shine; nothing could stop us from our games.

You Still Owe Me

IN 1954, THE NEW YORK GIANTS baseball team won the National League pennant and faced the Cleveland Indians, who had won the American League pennant, in the World Series. The Indians had won 111 games that year and were heavily favored to win it all.

"What odds will you give me if I take the Giants to sweep in four straight?" I asked my friend, who lived a few blocks away and went to a different school.

"I'll give you ten to one," he said, which I accepted.

Well, the Giants won the first game and I made sure he knew about it. Then, they won their second straight, which was getting good, because the ten-to-one bet was that they would win four in a row and sweep Cleveland. They were halfway home! My friend gave me ten-to-one odds that the Giants wouldn't sweep Cleveland, and I took that chance. Finally, when the Giants did sweep the Indians, I went over to his house to collect my winnings, but he stayed hidden in his room and wouldn't come out. I never saw him again. His mother kept telling me he was sick in his room and didn't feel good that day. I never collected the bet and never saw him again. I heard he became the drummer for the Cleveland Symphony, and I wonder if he ever made a bet again.

RICHARD G. KRASSEN

Love Them Phillies

BEFORE THE PHILADELPHIA PHILLIES baseball park changed its name to Connie Mack Stadium, it was called Shibe Park, located at 21st and Lehigh Avenues. The area was not the safest in the city at that time. At night, when you drove there to park your car, it would be dark, there would be trees hanging, and very little light. We sometimes found a local kid and paid him 50 cents to watch our car, to make sure nobody did it any harm.

Those were the days of gas wars, when local stations competed to see who could offer better prices. We paid 13.9 cents a gallon at an Esso station on the corner of Bustleton and Cottman Avenues, and we will surely never see prices like that again!

I first went to Shibe Park with my father, and later with friends. The Phillies would lose most of the time. We loved Shibe Park. One Sunday, we saw a flock of pigeons sitting on the rafters, which were built to hold up the park and make sure nothing collapsed.

One of the birds let fly a stream of birdshit onto a man dressed in a powder blue suit, and we waited to see how he would react. He took off his jacket, examined the fresh excrement on it, folded it neatly into a ball, placed it under his seat, and continued watching the game, completely unruffled by this avian assault on his clothes.

Del Ennis was one of my favorite Phillies. He went to Olney High School and took a bus to Shibe Park for a tryout. After a brief minor league career, he came up to the bigs as an official member of the Phillies. Del Ennis wore number fourteen and played left field most of the time, with an occasional game in right. He was a muscular guy, ponderous in the outfield and running the bases, and was greatly criticized by the Philadelphia fans—unduly, I would say. Del hit a lot of home runs, had a lot of RBIs, and was a major help in winning the 1950 National League pennant for the Phillies. When he would strike out, he would hear a tremendous amount of booing. People wanted him to hit it out of the park every time. There was just no leniency among those die-hard Philadelphia fans, but Del never said one negative thing about the fans.

One night, my father took me to a twilight double header when the Phillies played the St. Louis Cardinals. In the first game, Richie Ashburn fouled off 13 straight pitches to start the game. My hero, Robin Roberts, was pitching for the Phillies, and they lost, three to two. Wally Moon hit an opposite field double against the wall and beat Roberts, which was a painful loss for all of us. In the second game, the Cardinals loaded the bases in the first inning. Someone lofted a fly to Del Ennis in right field. Del, for reasons I never fully understood, tried to make what's called a basket catch. Instead of putting his hands up with the glove and catching it, he tried to have the ball come into his glove above his belt buckle. Willie Mays did this on a regular basis, but Del (no offense) was no Willie Mays. Anyway, with everybody running with two outs, Del dropped the ball and three runs scored. As Del ran to the dugout, every one of the 25,000 people was booing him unmercifully.

In the bottom of the first inning, the Phillies loaded the bases, and Del Ennis came up. On the first pitch, he took a ball low and almost in the dirt and hit it on the roof in Shibe Park's left field. As he ran around the bases, having hit a grand slam to make up for that big fat error earlier that inning, everyone stood up and cheered. Del Ennis will always be a hero of mine.

Stan Lopata was the Phillies catcher. He had what was called a peek-a-boo stance, where he would crouch down and look in at the pitcher as he pointed toward third base.

The Giants had a pitcher named Ruben Gomez. The first two

times Lopata came up that Sunday, Gomez threw the first ball right over the plate and struck him out soon after. I was 10 or 12 years old, but I ran to the top of the stands and yelled out as loud as I could to Stan Lopata.

"Swing at the first pitch! He's gonna throw it down the middle."

I don't know if he heard me, probably not, or thought of it himself, he probably did, but a few seconds after I yelled that to him, Stan Lopata hit the first pitch on the roof over the field for a home run. Bang! Home run!

I have so many good memories from Shibe Park with my friends and my father.

Hello, Girls!

I WENT TO WILSON JUNIOR HIGH SCHOOL for grades seven through nine. I became awakened to girls during this time and was perplexed by their effect on me. At the time, it was popular for girls to wear tight sweaters, like Lana Turner and some other famous movie actresses. This meant that the girls' breasts were quite noticeable and became quite a distraction for boys of that age.

I'm sure I wasn't the only one affected by the sensation of seeing the girls like this, and I was not the only boy afflicted with constant erections in school. In fact, it got so bad that when a teacher would call on people to stand up and answer questions, I was always worried that if I stood up I would be embarrassed, because everyone would see my erection. I would think there are plenty of men out there who can relate to this "problem."

My Biggest Fan

MY FATHER ATTENDED all of my basketball games at Wilson Junior High School. In my senior year, we played 15 games and won 14 of them. Once, against Stoddard Fleischer, he had to keep score because the man who normally did that job was ill, and my dad volunteered. For reasons still unexplained, when the officials went over the score at the end of the game, we lost by one point because my father missed recording a basket. He always worried that he had messed up our perfect season. Many years later, a friend told me that my father asked him if I had ever said anything to him about my father messing up our season, and he said no.

My father died suddenly when I was 44. I never told him how important it was to me that he came to all of my games. The truth is, on the final play of that game, I had tried to drive to the basket and was called for charging, and we lost by one. We beat that same team, Stoddard Fleischer, by 15 points at home two weeks later.

Phil Golden was the basketball coach at Wilson. He had played basketball as a kid. He was a nice, soft spoken man. In eighth grade, I was playing intramurals when a teacher told Phil Golden about me, and he put me on the team. In ninth grade, I became the captain and high scorer, and we won every game except one.

Phillip Golden treated me almost like I was his son. He was always kind and helpful. During one game when I wasn't playing well, he took me out and scolded me because I was taking too many shots. He did it in a nice way.

When Phil had a 90th birthday party, of all the people that he had taught and had contact with, those he coached and knew, he only invited two people to his party besides his family. I was fortunate to be one of them, but sadly I couldn't go, as I had a prior commitment outside the country. He kept asking me if I was coming, but he didn't understand that I had previous plans. He passed on a year or two later. I'm sad that I didn't get to that party, because I knew how much he wanted me there; I'll never forget how nicely he treated me.

When I played on that team at Wilson Junior High, we often promoted our games at assemblies, where we appeared in our uniforms to talk to the students, so they'd come to our games.

One time, when an assembly ran long, I was late for my English class. Ms. Stockton asked her class where I was. They told her I was on the basketball team and at the assembly. Apparently, she told the class that she knew people like me who were student-athletes, and they wound up cutting lettuce in the supermarket. She thought that's what their life would turn out to be.

She was close, because as it turns out I wound up selling life insurance for a living—a little different than lettuce, but still a life of pain *without* sports.

When it came time for my large class to graduate, Wilson Junior High School presented its most prestigious award, the American Legion Award, which was given for character and other outstanding qualities. There were so many of us onstage they had to seat some of the kids in the first two rows of the audience. I was seated on the end of the second row. There were several boring speeches, which made me doze off a little, and then they got to the presentation of the American Legion Award.

I was practically asleep when they called my name. The boy next to me punched me in the arm.

"That's you, they called you. Go up there."

I woke up there and accepted that American Legion Award. I don't know why I got it, probably because I played basketball for the school and they charged admission to get into the games, and we had a good team, so they made some money from it. I know that my coach, Phil Golden, really liked me and probably nominated me. I cherished that award and was glad to receive it in junior high school.

I never looked at myself as being special, because I was never a great student. Malcolm, a good friend of mine, told me that the president of the class's mother was upset and complained to him about me receiving the award.

"My son did not get the award. Why did Richard Krassen? He's just an athlete. Why didn't *my* son get the award?"

Her son and I were friends! He never said anything, but his mother felt that her son should have gotten the award because he was the president of the class and a good student, certainly better than me. Her son, Jay, became an orthopedic surgeon, so maybe she was right.

That's What Friends Are For?

MY TWO CLOSEST FRIENDS in junior high school were Fred Kauffman, who is still my closest friend and lives in Florida, and Mel Kaulkin, who lives near Penn State right now. Every once in a while, when we were in class, someone would let go a fart, and we used to grade them as to their power when it came to loudness and overall foul-smelling quality.

After a lot of consideration, we came to the conclusion that Melvin's fart in social studies was not the loudest, but it was surely the most devastating. People from all corners of the classroom turned their heads, asking if anybody knew the source of such a foul smell. Fred, Mel, and I kept a straight face, which was not easy at all to do.

When I close my eyes now and take a whiff, I can almost smell that awful aroma from Melvin's fart. Fred did cut an epic fart in hygiene class, which was very loud and powerful, but it did not have the foul odor of Mel's, so we had to give Fred second place on that.

Home Away from Home

THE J HAMPTON PLAYGROUND became the scene of some legendary pick-up games on its basketball court. That's where my best friend Fred Kauffman and I played a lot of hoops and fiercely-fought games of stickball.

I met Alan Tunick there. We became friendly, and he urged me to become a member of the cross-country team in 10th grade. We trained and ran races in the fall season. Practicing after school was something I could never get excited about, as I always knew there was probably more fun to be had at the local playground and I was missing it, running and running and essentially getting nowhere. Maybe that's because I was a mediocre long-distance runner.

Every week we had a meet at Belmont Plateau, racing against a group of other Philadelphia-area schools. I tried during the regular season, but my times never rose above the middle of the pack.

Then came the championships—the one race of the year that really counted. I was entered in the junior varsity cadet classification. The turning point for me came when I asked Jim Popowski for a favor. He had just finished running in the junior high race.

"Could I borrow your running shoes?" I asked him. I expected a rejection, but he surprised me by agreeing to loan me his shoes.

In all my previous races I had run in hi-top sneakers, which were meant for playing basketball. I was quick enough on the court, but they only slowed me down on the cross- country trails, where I was already too darn slow. His official running shoes were so light! As soon as I put them on and jogged a few yards I felt like I was running barefoot. I flew around the course and knocked a full minute off my time. I finished 25th in that race against all the runners from all the schools in the city.

Our coach was impressed. He gave me a JV letter, which I was proud to own. However, for some reason still unclear, I never ran cross-country again. Al was a much better runner than me and he ran varsity. Mike Braude, who became a friend at Penn, ran varsity for Central High School. I remember one runner racing with a Bible. He was a top runner, so I guess God made him faster. In my case, a Bible would not have helped me. I needed more practice and dedication, but I was not up to it.

I always preferred my home away from home on the playgrounds of my neighborhood.

Dribble, Not Draw

IT'S IMPORTANT TO KNOW that all of us have our strengths and weaknesses, and we should recognize what they are. One glaring weakness of mine, among many, is that I'm not very good with my hands at making things, which I realized at a young age.

My first experience was in mechanical drawing. I had a teacher named Russ Ellis. He would put these things on the board and we'd have to copy them, using a T-square and a protractor. I didn't know how to use any of those instruments very well. We were supposed to create stuff, and I would like to thank Martin Kaufield, who sat next to me and helped me. Thank you, Martin.

He would do his work in about three minutes.

"Martin, could you please do one for me?"

He was nice and did mine, too. That's how I got through it. I would have failed the course for sure without him. I had no ability and no concept of how things were done in that arena. I just didn't.

Woodshop with Mr. Anderson was not much better. We had to make a broom holder, and I kept screwing it up. Finally, Mr. Anderson got so angry and annoyed with me that he took the wood and made it himself. I turned it in, and he gave himself a C. I could never understand why Mr. Anderson did that, since he built it, but I think it might have been the fact that he actually built the whole thing for me pretty much, while I watched. He factored in an A for him and an F for me and came up with a C. Nice guy.

Jim Forscythe was my metal shop teacher. We used a soldering iron that took on different colors when it got hot. It was fun just to watch it change colors. We were supposed to make cookie cutters, using what was called flux, which is a glue that went between the cookie-cutter parts.

"After you make the cookie-cutter with the flux," Jim Forscythe said to us, "it should be so tight, if you did it right, that I should not be able to pull it apart."

After four or five weeks, I finally made a cookie cutter that held together. I was so sloppy at first, and honestly, I just didn't care that much about any of it. I wasn't in to it at all. The first time Mr. Forscythe went around to each child and pulled on their cookie-cutter to see if he could pull them apart, most everybody had theirs just right, and he couldn't pull it apart. When he came to me and pulled on mine, it all came apart. He threw it on the floor.

"Krassen, F."

Art class was just as bad. That's when I realized I had absolutely zero artistic talent. Our teacher, Mrs. Sauer, said, "I will never keep you off the honor roll for art. I don't feel that art should do that."

At the end of the term, I had two Cs. You were only allowed one C in a minor, plus if you had all As and Bs you got on the honor roll. I had two Cs, one in wood shop and one in art. I went up to Ms. Sauer and said, "Ms. Sauer, do you remember at the beginning of class, you said that you would never keep me off the honor roll because of art?"

"Yes I do," she said.

"Well, here's my report card. Have a look."

"I see you got two Cs, Richard."

"Yes, but my other teacher never said he would keep me off of the honor roll if I got a C with him."

Ms. Sour looked at me quite upset.

"Okay. I will honor my word."

She changed me from a C to a B. I'm sure she regretted what she said for the rest of her career—giving someone so inept like me a B, someone who surely deserved at most a C, just to honor what she told me. I did keep her to her word and was able to fight for something I wanted and had been promised. The whole episode was a big life lesson.

I took another art class with Mrs. Long, where we carved soap.

"You'll take the soap and carve an animal out of it," she said.

Somebody made a little squirrel and someone else made a little dog. I kept cutting the soap and it just kept getting smaller and smaller because I kept doing it wrong. I held up this little piece of soap and said to Mrs. Long, "This is an ant." She looked at me with disdain, and that disgusted look on her face when she saw my work was not pleasant at all. It was clear once again, to me and everyone else, that I had absolutely no talent or ability in art, to go along with my lack of ability in shop and a lot of other things one does with their hands.

One day, my friend, Danny, had an epileptic fit right there in art class and fell off his chair in front of me. Calmly and coolly, Miss Long stuck a small ruler into his mouth so he would not bite his tongue while she secured a passageway for him to breath. The ambulance came; Danny was okay and returned to school the next day. Mrs. Long will always be my hero, even though she made it perfectly clear how inept I was as an art student. She was so right.

My wife is a very talented artist. I married her for those artistic abilities, and much more.

My First Car

WHEN I WAS SIXTEEN YEARS OLD, my father taught me how to drive in his Rocket Oldsmobile, which I loved. The first time I went for my driving test, I backed up over the curb and failed. The second time, I passed. My father, who was not the greatest person around cars, said he would look for a car for my mother and me to share.

We met a private owner of a 1953 green Chevy Bel Air. Four or five people had bought it before us over a three-year span, which should have tipped us off that maybe there was a problem with the car. It was a standard transmission with a clutch, which I learned to operate in driver's ed class in high school.

The car ended up in the shop as much as it was on the road, because it was what's called an eleven, meaning it was constantly breaking down. When it was working, I was able to drive it to school, and my mother drove it on certain days, so we did kind of split it.

We all remember our first car, and I have fond memories of mine, even though it was in the shop so often.

Out on a Limb

DURING TENTH GRADE, I had an English teacher named Ms. Granoff. She gave everyone a book report to write, for a day in the future when she would call on you. For reasons I can't explain, partially because I didn't like to do homework at that point in my life, I walked into class on the day of doing my book report totally unprepared. I had not read the book, and I had to sit down and write a book report.

Maybe my proudest achievement in school was what I faced that day, when I created a book called *Southpaw from Saint Louis*, about a person who overcame a physical disability and went on to become an outstanding pitcher.

I wound up getting one of the highest marks in the class for the book report. I considered that a crowning achievement, although I wouldn't recommend it for anybody in the future.

Pass or Fail Is Fine with Me

TOM CAREY WAS THE STARTING SHORTSTOP on the baseball team that won the city championship. He was a kicker and split-end on the football team, too, and he played JV basketball and varsity ball with me during our junior year, although we didn't get much playing time that year.

I had a teacher in tenth grade named Mrs. Rabin. I had a C in her class, a very high C, bordering on a B.

"Richard, if you go home tonight and do a report and bring it back tomorrow and tell the class something that interests you and it's written well, I will bring your grade up to a B. Right now, you are on the border."

I went home and looked at the paper. There were two science fiction movies I really wanted to see at a big theater in Center City. I picked up the phone and called my friend, Tom Carey.

"Tom, instead of going to school tomorrow, would you like to go into town with me to see these two movies?"

"Sure," said Tom.

He was a big science fiction lover. Later he became famous studying UFOs in New Mexico. He's written books about it.

We went into town and enjoyed the double feature. The next morning, Mrs. Rabin confronted me.

"Richard, where were you yesterday?"

"I couldn't make it in."

"Okay, then. You're going to get a C."

"Okay."

Evidently at that time, and probably for most of my academic career, for reasons I don't really understand, grades never seemed to be a big priority for me. I would've been fine with pass or fail.

I guess there were lots of things to do that seemed to be a lot more fun than — like bowling. It was one of the things my friends and I used to enjoy doing outside of high school, besides cruising and eating, which was popular in those days.

If you went at midnight, you could bowl all night for like $3 or maybe $5. All night! Sometimes, we would actually go to a bowling alley in the Mayfair section of town and bowl from twelve o'clock till maybe three in the morning before staggering home.

That was an integral part of our teenaged entertainment.

Making Up My Own Mind for a Change

IN THE MIDDLE OF ELEVENTH GRADE at Lincoln High School, most the friends I grew up with, who were mostly Jewish, were in school with me. A new Northeast High School had just been built closer to our neighborhood, and all of my friends were going to go there. It was going to be their school, just for them, friendly to their identity, but I decided to stay at Lincoln. I played basketball there, and that made me happy. I made an independent decision, not based on my friends or what everybody else was doing, but on what I felt was right for me.

This was another life lesson—that everybody should do what feels right for them and not get sucked up in what everybody else is doing. It was a decision I made strictly on my own, without my parents. That was that.

I was on the varsity basketball team in my junior and senior years. In my junior year, I did not play, because I wasn't good enough. I sat on the bench when we went to the Palestra and lost to Overbrook High School. During my senior year, I was having a problem with my foot. Every time I would jump and come down I got a sharp pain on the ball of my foot. I didn't know what it was; I would just squeeze it when I sat down, and it would be fine, but the pain kept me from jumping, and I missed a lot of practices.

In my senior year, we had a new coach, Harry Silcox, who had been a fine basketball player at Temple University, including a 26-point game in a one-point victory over Tom Gola and a great Lasalle team. Unbeknownst to me, I was supposed to be cut on a rainy Friday afternoon, because I had shown him nothing, and he had no reason to keep me. On that Friday, though, I did two significant things: I blocked a shot by Fred Schmidt, one of the best players in the city who was on our team, and when my teammate, Tony Shepherd, overplayed me to trying to steal the ball, I went back door on him, got a pass, and scored.

Mr. Silcox was impressed.

"Richard, I had you cut from the team, but you showed me some good things today. I'm going to leave you on."

"Mr. Silcox, I think I'm going to help this team at some point."

I sat on the bench and started in a preseason game; a ball hit my index finger and thumb, and I couldn't move my hand.

"I can't move my hand, coach."

He put in Allen Flexer, a friend of mine. Allen later became president of The Spectrum, the legendary sporting and concert arena in Philadelphia.

"Mr. Silcox, is there a problem?" I said to him later in the hall.

"Well, I didn't think you wanted to play."

"What do you mean?"

"Well, when I played for Temple against Kentucky, I broke my nose and I played with a mask."

I tried to figure out what playing with a mask in college had to do with me not being able to catch the ball or dribble or shoot in a preseason game in high school in Philadelphia.

Another disappointing incident occurred later in a game, when there was a breakaway layup by one of the other players. I chased him down and stopped him, then fell to the ground. The coach just walked by me without saying a word. I felt like he could have at least come over and said "nice play" or helped pick me up.

We were undefeated in my senior year while I was riding the bench, along with four other guys. When we played Central High School, one of the fellows on our team got so angry that he took the basketball and threw it on the ground; it went up into the ceiling, and he was thrown out of the game. Harry Silcox looked down the bench and realized I was the only person big enough to put in.

"Krassen," he said, waving for me to get out there.

I noticed him put his hands on his head as if to say, "Woe is me, this is the end."

By some miracle, I played well and held the leading scorer on the other team to two points in the second half. We won the game, and I started every game from then on.

During the last game of the season, we played Frankford High School on a Saturday morning, and it was like I never woke up. I didn't score, and I played an awful game, I threw a ball away on the last play of the game, and we lost at the buzzer.

The next game, we were scheduled to play Overbrook High School in the playoffs at the Palestra. Mr. Silcox had removed me from the starting team, but that week in practice, I played my way back and was able to start against the legendary Overbrook High School at the Palestra in Philadelphia. They had Wali Jones, Walt Hazzard, Richie Richman, Wayne Hightower, and Ralph Hayward. Four of them wound up playing pro basketball.

We froze the ball because there was no 24-second clock, which meant we could keep the ball away from them. I made a jump shot and two foul shots in the first four minutes and thirty-five seconds of the game, so I had four points, and nobody else had any. I wound up being our high scorer in that game with seven points, but we lost 44-22. That was a memorable moment to play against such amazing players from Overbrook in that famous arena.

Wali Jones remains a legend to people who have followed basketball in Philadelphia over the last sixty-five years. He was the main man on his championship high school team at Overbrook, and that team is still considered to be one of the top five city high school teams in Philadelphia history.

Wali went on to be a star player at Villanova University. Once he reached the NBA, he became an integral piece of the 1967 world championship, won by our hometown 76ers. Wali, rated 65th among the greatest Sixers in history by an online basketball source, gives us much to ponder about his basketball career.

Players such as Wilt Chamberlain, Chet Walker, Luke Jackson, Billy Cunningham, Hal Greer, and Larry Costello are all deservedly in the top 30. Why is Wali #65? For more than 25 years, the 1967 team was considered by most to be the best NBA team of all time.

Who made the biggest shots to win that title? Wali.

Who was the go-to man in the close-out game against the Celtics? Wali.

He made six shots in the face of the legendary Sam Jones to bring us back to victory. In game five at home against the San Francisco Warriors, the team went cold in the second half and lost. In game six, Wali had 27 points and led the team to a three-point win in the clinching fourth game.

Wali was the man.

He has been a winner his whole life, and in my opinion, deserves to be in the top 30. I was fortunate enough to reconnect with Wali through a mutual friend. I recently went to the Wright Community Center on Haverford Avenue and took a picture with him and Ken Hamilton. Ken coached at Ben Franklin High School for 28 seasons and won 456 games and four championships. Pooh Richardson was one of his players.

Wali worked in the Miami Heat organization for more than 20 years and now conducts non-profit basketball clinics for kids. He stresses reading, which I firmly support. In fact, I would like to help him at his clinics in Philadelphia in any capacity they need.

Wali's father, who is 102 years old now, still lives right here in Philadelphia, and Wali visits him whenever he comes to town from his home in Florida.

I am proud to call Wali my friend.

Fit for a King

ON FRIDAY AND SATURDAY NIGHTS, my friends and I used to cruise the neighborhood. We were about 16 and didn't know what else to do with ourselves, so we cruised. That was our big social life. We would go to places like the Tyson Grill and get a steak sandwich and a cherry coke, and maybe fries. We would go to Linton's, on Castor Avenue and Hellerman, and get a bacon, lettuce, and tomato sandwich. The most interesting thing about Linton's was the conveyor belt, where you would actually see the food that you ordered, almost like a sliding board, coming down at you, and you would recognize your food as it approached.

I also went quite often to Horn & Hardart's, with my friends and my parents. We'd get a Salisbury steak and a pot of baked beans, or macaroni and a fish cake. This was an automat, so if you wanted a roll and butter, you'd go up to the machine, put a nickel in, open the door, and out came your food. I got a Salisbury steak for 25 cents, a pot of baked beans for 15 cents, and maybe spinach or macaroni or something else for 10 cents. That would be plenty; for 50 cents or 75 cents, you could eat like a king.

I also remember Nedick's, where you got a hotdog and an orange drink, which was kind of diluted, but tasted good because it had a lot of sugar in it. The hotdogs were not good at all, but I thought they were at the time. We also went to the Hot Shop on Broad and Godfrey and got awful hamburgers, which we also thought were good. Sometimes, we cruised around and ended up at a girl's house;

we'd promise after talking to them awhile that we'd call them, but of course, we never did. Who knows why?

One time, I met a girl and told her I'd call her.

"Will you call me, really?"

"Uh, yeah, sure I will."

I never did. Six months later, I saw her at a function, walked up to her and she walked away from me. She was angry because I had told her I would call her. I don't know why I didn't call her after I told her I would. It's like today, when many people tell me they're going to call me to buy insurance and they never call. I guess that's some kind of payback for what I did to this young girl at an early age. I think I'm being punished for that, and I understand.

We also went to the Palestra at the University of Pennsylvania to watch basketball games. They had double and triple-headers, which we enjoyed very much.

I liked ushering at Franklin Field in 1958 and 1959, when I worked all of the University of Pennsylvania home football games. I received exactly one dollar per game to use a rag and wipe down the seats before the games. I was an usher for the Philadelphia Eagles, too, during those two years, which allowed me to earn a few extra bucks. Sadly, I didn't get to usher in 1960 when the Eagles won the NFL championship, but I did win 50 cents betting on the game with some old camp friends in Teaneck, New Jersey.

I ushered at the Palestra in 1957 and 1958, when I drove to the venue after my own basketball practice and received a $2 stipend for gas and food. I saw Jerry West playing for the University of West Virginia, when he dropped 37 points against Villanova.

That was how we spent our late teenaged years before going off to college. Between drive-in restaurants, drive-in movies, and sports, we kept busy doing nothing. And back then, that kind of nothing was just fine and dandy for us.

The Big O

WOMEN AND BASKETBALL JUST DON'T MIX, especially for a boy in his senior year of high school. One day in Mr. Haar's social studies class, I was enjoying flirting with a couple of girls and felt really flattered to have their attention. One of the girls asked me to accompany her to a wedding reception, and I immediately said yes. My friend, Fred, went along with the other girl, which made it a dream double date.

That same night, I was supposed to work as an usher at the Palestra for a game featuring the one and only Oscar Robertson, when his fantastic University of Cincinnati team came to town to play Temple University.

This was a dream come true for me—to see the Big O in the Palestra. Unfortunately, I was also dreaming about having a great time with my date and didn't plan my time well at all. As it turned out, I missed seeing Oscar, and the reception was boring.

We finally left the two girls there, but it was too late to get to the game. What a jerk! Women are lethal, and I really learned that lesson later in life when I got divorced. For a high school boy in love with basketball, missing the chance to see Oscar Robertson play is something I still regret.

Jazz

AT AGES 16 AND 17, I drove during the week to Peps and the Show Boat by myself, because none of my friends were interested in hearing jazz, which was my passion at the time. I was big for my age, so no one ever carded me. I had to buy a drink, so I ordered scotch and nursed it for two sets. Very few people attended during the week, so I got a close-up view of legends, such as Miles Davis, Junior Mance, Dinah Washington, Joe Williams, and Ray Bryant. I saw all the greats, because the 1950s was a great decade for jazz.

I was sitting at Peps one evening when a really massive guy came in and sat next to me.

"Good evening, Mr. Liston," said the bartender.

Huh?

Sonny Liston?

I gulped down my drink, pretended not to notice, and continued listening to the music I loved.

Leadership

CHARLES WILLIAMS WAS MY PRINCIPAL at Lincoln High School. I learned a lot about leadership from him. He was a very fair man who commanded respect. I believe he was a military veteran, had graduated from Brown University, and was very intelligent. One thing I admired about Mr. Williams was that when we had an assembly and he would stand up to speak, he invariably stopped almost every time there was noise among the students. He had an eagle eye to pick out the source of the sound.

"That young man in the eighteenth row in the green shirt," he would say, "please stand up and go to my office right now and wait for me."

Everyone would be very quiet and attentive from then on, because no one wanted to be called out to go to his office and speak to him about talking or being disrespectful. It was effective leadership, and I greatly respected that.

One day, we had a terrible snowfall and for want of anything better to do, I went to school, even though it was difficult to get there. Mr. Williams called everybody who had showed up, which weren't many, into the auditorium.

"I want to commend everybody who came into school today, because it shows a certain character and dedication to learning."

He gave accolades to everyone who went to school, which was a nice thing to do. It just shows that leadership is important in schools and in all walks of life.

When I graduated, Mr. Williams called me into his office. He knew that I played basketball and that my grades were pretty good.

"Richard, how would you like it if I wrote you a nice recommendation for you to go to Brown University?"

"Thank you very much, Mr. Williams, let me think about it."

As it turned out I did not apply to Brown, but it was a really nice gesture on his part, which meant a lot to me.

What's a Career Path?

THE NICEST THING ABOUT MY MOTHER was that she gave me so much latitude and freedom. Although many parents today give tremendous amounts of attention to their children, to my mind that can be good and bad. My mother didn't always ask me about my assignments or grades or how I was doing, so I lived my life as I saw fit. My friends, mostly Jewish, had career paths they discussed with their parents—to be a dentist, a doctor, or an accountant—but none of that was ever discussed in my house.

By the time I graduated from high school, the only thing that mattered to me was music and sports. I never thought about my future, never gave a thought to what I'd do after school, about getting married, or making a living. I was living strictly in the moment, trying to find things that I enjoyed. And there was a price to pay for that later in my life . . .

My father also never brought up these issues. There was no real discussion about any of it, and no real closeness between my parents and me. We had no meaningful conversation about what I felt, why I might have been upset about something, or what I aspired to do with my life. In fact, my parents got into a big argument one night because they were discussing what I was going to do after I got out of school, as if it were a big question mark. I overheard them.

"He can do the insurance business with me," my father said.

"Richard is not a salesman," said my mother. "He doesn't like small talk; he's not a back slapper, and he's not particularly aggressive with people. He just doesn't have any of the traits that you really need to be a salesman."

I was still winging it in high school. From her perspective, my mother was right about me at that time in my life. That's not necessarily a bad thing. I eventually evolved to gain a little more confidence and a little more assertiveness.

I applied to four colleges: Temple, University of Pennsylvania, Penn State, and Lafayette. I had talked to my coach, Harry Silcox, about a possible scholarship to Temple. He told me I wasn't good enough for that level of competition, and I agreed with him. I went up to Lafayette, talked to them, and they had some interest in me. They were going to give me some grants and financial aid. Then they saw my father's Oldsmobile outside.

"Is that your Oldsmobile, Mr. Krassen?"

He said it was. They asked if it was paid for, and he nodded.

"You're not going to get any grant or aid from Lafayette," they told me.

That was the end of that.

It came down to Penn State and University of Pennsylvania's Wharton School. I was going to go to Penn State, because I had lived in Philadelphia my whole life and thought Penn State would be a different, appealing environment. I felt flattered, though, that I was accepted at Penn, because it has such an excellent reputation. However, I think I was intimidated and worried that I'd have trouble there, because I really didn't see myself as a person who studied very much or was academic enough to compete with the people attending Penn. It just seemed a little over the top to me. I was ready to go to Penn State, but after staying up all night I decided to go to Penn, which I never regretted.

What a Wonderful World

LOOKING BACK OVER THE FIRST EIGHTEEN years of my life, one thing that stands out is a feeling of isolation, of loneliness and an unwelcome solitude. Although I had some good friends, my life at home with my parents was lonely, as they were constantly occupied. We didn't discuss any meaningful subjects, and it seemed to me like many of my friends had a defined path they figured out with the support of their families. That led them to a relatively healthy social life, too. I had some interest in the opposite sex, but I was too scared and unsure of myself to do anything about it.

I had a strong sense of isolation and feeling alone. Although my parents gave me a long leash to be on my own, it can a double-edged sword, because it's tough to go through life by yourself, without any mentoring or help.

I always did my homework, until I started liking basketball so much and basically stopped doing homework. I did enough to get by, but I could have done a better job of studying and learning.

I was nervous heading to Penn, because I would be competing with top students from Philadelphia and all over the country. At that time, Penn may have been considered the weakest of the Ivy League schools, but it was still formidable, especially to me.

I continue to be fascinated even today with how much my childhood has influenced my adult life. The culture I grew up in—at home, in school, and on the streets and courts and fields of my neighborhood—have had so much influence on who I became as a young man and how I am living today as an old one.

Thank God for Philadelphia.

Spring to Life

Baseballs sailing through the air,
Fathers and sons finding time to share,
Emerging flowers add an artful flare,
Chirping birds complete the bill of fare.

How many dreams do we have lying dormant,
Failing to bloom, our smiles in torment,
A plan for happiness we must carefully foment,
To taste some of life's pure magic moments.

Like the beautiful butterfly,
Our true spirit must fly free,
To be the best human being,
We can possibly be.

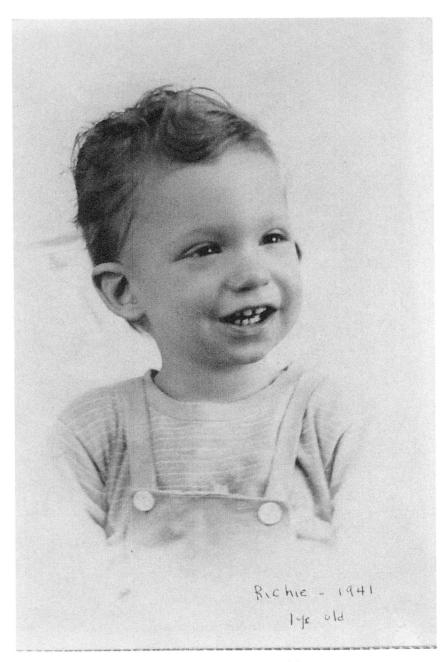

Here I am, one year old.

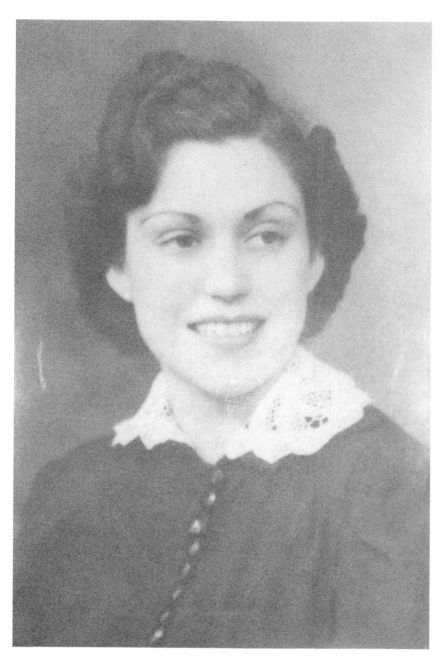

My mother.

In the neighborhood as a young boy.

My parents, Vera and Morris.

Elementary years.

Ann Karchin.

Played wire ball on these street wires, corner of Knorr and Kindred.

Games of step ball were played here, at 6749 Kindred St.

My home from 1943 to 1953, 6749 Kindred St.

Here I am, at my Bar Mitzvah, with my sister, Ellen.

My second home, from 1953 to 1964, at 6704 Large Street.

Wilson Junior High School, grades 7 to 9.

I wish I'd been that tall.

My patented hook shot.

Niagara Falls, 1954.

PART TWO

Leaving the Nest and Creating My Own

A Love Affair Continues

WHEN IT COMES TO MY YOUNGER, smarter, handsomer self, my childhood essentially ended in the spring of 1958. That's when I became a free agent, not exactly past my days of youthful adolescence, and not sure if I was ready for living on my own at the University of Pennsylvania.

The thought of going there in the fall to enroll in the Wharton School felt a little intimidating. I still had poor listening skills and shaky study habits. I would be competing with other freshman and upperclassmen at the top or near the top of their class.

My summer priority became getting a job and having some fun. When I secured a job in Atlantic City, New Jersey, I figured both would be accomplished. Luckily, Aunt Sadie, my mother's older sister, knew a man named Herman, who worked as a captain at The Shelbourne Hotel dining room in Atlantic City.

I lived nearby with a boyhood pal, Arnie Ghen, in a fleabag room on New York Avenue. We shared a spartan existence, as both of us were saving money for college, which was getting closer.

The atmosphere in the hotel restaurant was quite fancy. There was a maître d, who dressed handsomely in a coat and tails. The captains wore blue jackets, and the waiters were decked out in elegant burgundy jackets.

The lowest class workers were the busboys, which, as a high school graduate with no real work experience, was exactly what I qualified for as a summer employee. That was fine with me. I got to wear a white cotton coat and black pants, and I enjoyed working in that get-up for my lunch and dinner shifts.

Actually, during my senior year of high school, I cut a week of classes to work as a busboy at The Breakers Hotel during the Jewish holiday of Passover. I had experience! Even so, I started in Atlantic City at the bottom.

The wages were almost nonexistent, but we made money on tips, which we received from a percentage of the waiters' income. We earned them by setting the tables and clearing the dirty dishes, so the better we did with those two tasks, the more we might make.

We also secured whatever condiments were requested by the waiters and guests and filled empty water glasses.

The other busboys and I earned additional money in another way. After all the guests were finished eating their dinners, the waiters were required to place a clean, fresh tablecloth on each table. They also had to position four to eight place settings on their assigned tables. We did this for them, and they traditionally tipped us, which added up pretty well over the course of the summer.

A few notable incidents occurred during my time working at the Shelbourne. I was once asked to put a fresh tablecloth and place setting on one waiter's table. Usually, that would be no problem, but at the moment there were no more large, clean tablecloths for his table of eight. I did the table of three that he needed done, because I had the tablecloths for that, but I had nothing for the big one.

The next morning, the waiter's station captain reprimanded him for not setting the table. The waiter was not happy with me, because in his mind I had let him down. I wish I would have washed the tablecloth and dried it and ironed it myself. I hated letting people down. That's just me, then and now, and even though it was impossible to launder a tablecloth while working, I still felt terrible for not doing my job perfectly.

I am still like that, and as a true Scorpio, I try to be trustworthy and reliable in everything I endeavor to do. Like all of us, however, I come up short sometimes, and I just have to deal with it.

Dealing with unexpected situations is a valuable lesson I learned that summer. The hotel dining room was beautiful. The entire hotel, located at Michigan Avenue and the boardwalk, was splendid. The carpeting was lush, and the lighting was exquisite and looked expensive. So were the prices on the menu, even for that time. The restaurant fed us dinner, and somehow managed to serve the worst food known to man. I don't know how they offered such a good menu to the customers and simultaneously fed us garbage, but they did! Prisoners all over the country would be rioting today if they were given this type of food. It was downright terrible!

There was a way to combat this. Most patrons would not finish their food. They would regularly leave lobster, lamb chops, or steak on their plates. As you cleared the table, you could take a napkin and cover the food while bringing it back to the kitchen.

I think the saying goes, "Once a scavenger, always a scavenger," and that applied to us. As soon as we figured out how things worked, we ate pretty well for the duration of the season.

Late in the summer, some of the Miss America contestants stayed in our hotel and ate there. Miss Kansas was beautiful (as if she were the only one in that category). She noticed me looking at her from time to time and smiled at me. Wow. That was exciting, but of course I never said boo to her.

One time, a captain asked me to get a new bottle of ketchup. The top was loose for some inexplicable reason, and as I was swinging my arms on the way back into the dining room, ketchup started flying everywhere. Luckily, I didn't get fired.

All summer long, if it wasn't one adventure to remember, it was another that didn't quite happen as we hoped but was memorable simply for its possibilities.

For example, a nice Italian waiter I bussed for on a regular basis kept telling me about his beautiful daughter back home in Philadelphia. Wow. Was he setting me up with Sophia Loren, perhaps? I couldn't wait to get home and meet her when our employment was completed after Labor Day.

As my luck would have it, she was nothing like what I had hoped for or expected. Let's just leave it like that. I realize that to my waiter friend, his daughter was the most beautiful girl in the world. There's something very sweet about that, and I hope all fathers feel the same way about their daughters.

All in all, it was a good summer, and I gladly returned home to Philadelphia, with cash in my pocket for school and a headful of anxiety about attending university.

Welcome to West Philadelphia

IN THE FALL OF 1958, tuition at the University of Pennsylvania was about $900 a year. Today, it's more than 50 times that amount. How can that be? The cost per class credit is mind-blowing and off the charts. What are students paying for? They used graduate students back then to teach basic courses at Wharton and in the general college, and they still do, now probably even more than before as the curriculum expands. Those young men attended graduate school for free and may have received a small stipend. They did the brunt of the teaching work, while the professors mainly showed up to deliver lectures. They were paid a competitive salary for the time, but nowhere near as much as their successors are paid these days.

Universities like Penn, which have become synonymous with non-profit corporations, have developed enormous endowments to support their many new projects and expenditures. This comes from small, medium, and large donations, which means the fundraising process goes on all year round.

Most colleges charge too much, especially the private ones. There is no rationale for why they are so expensive. It seems to be a question of supply and demand. As the 12th most desirable school in the country, according to the latest research I could find, Penn is an attractive destination, and its rising costs reflect that. People want to go there, maybe even more for its reputation than the education it offers. Parents of aspiring applicants must be wealthy enough to afford the tuition and room and board or relatively poor enough to qualify for a scholarship and/or financial aid. Families in the middle often end up piling up huge debts from student loans.

In 1958, The University of Pennsylvania was considered a safety school for aspiring Ivy League applicants. The school admitted many local students to help build up its scholastic grade point average—top-notch scholars from city schools and the suburbs. My two friends, Walter Brown and Alan Gart, were among the top students who received scholarships.

At Wharton, the grading scale was very rigid. An 'A' required scores of 93 to 100. A 'B' was 85 to 92. A 'C' came with a 77 to 84, and 70 to 76 meant you received a 'D'.

Anything under a 70 spelled failure. The scale for general college courses was looser. In order to graduate, you had to receive more Cs than Ds, which meant you needed about a 75 to make it across the finish line. I knew several people who flunked out.

During one semester of my sophomore year, I got 3 Ds and almost ended my days at Penn. I flunked statistics 1B and had to take it over. My heart was never in it, much less my mind. I had no passion or genuine desire to learn most of what they were teaching. Some of the courses were interesting, but most were not.

I took four history courses one semester because I liked history. I also liked English Literature. Landon Burns, a Yale graduate, was our teacher. One of the books was *Catcher in the Rye*. I liked the rebellion it portrayed. Most of my teachers were good at accumulating information but sorely lacking in how they presented it. Since I was always in my head, full of anxiety and too many questions, I needed a captivating personality as my teacher to get me to listen and absorb the information they were providing. Unfortunately, at least for me, they were few and far between.

I never came close to getting a single 'A' in my four years at Penn. I remember walking past the library nearly every day, but I was only inside it once in four years.

Most of my friends, who were Jewish, had career goals to become doctors, dentists, lawyers, CPAs, and engineers. Me? I was lost. I had no goals. I was not thinking about my future at all. Instead, I was merely going through the motions, which I soon found out could be a real problem. If you are fortunate enough to find a passion that can produce a good income and be beneficial for the people you are serving, then you have hit life's lottery jackpot. Back then, I was very far from that.

During a mechanical drawing class in seventh grade, I had a T-square in my hand, which I did not like using at all. I said to myself that I hoped I could find something one day that I would love and could be successful at. My complete ineptitude in mechanical drawing class brought that to my attention, and I never forgot how that felt and the lesson of those times.

Back in my sophomore year at college, when I came close to flunking out, it made me wonder why wasn't reading the textbooks. They were boring, but I knew that I needed to read them in order to pass the classes. Still, I resisted, and the reasons for that remain mystifying. Was I being a real idiot, or just lazy, or what?

I could not swim when I first entered college. They told me that if I did not learn to swim and meet the requirements of the class, then I would not graduate. Wow. They were not kidding! Time to learn to swim. I ended up doing 24 laps in 30 minutes in the deep end without touching the sides. I did it! I am a highly anxious person, and things like swimming with correct breathing techniques in the water are a challenge for me.

In the late 50s and early 60s, the surrounding neighborhood in West Philadelphia was not attractive at all. All the restaurants, like Al's Penn House, were third-rate. The food looked and tasted two levels below comfort food, if that's even possible in a first-world country. Dietrich Hall, where I attended my Wharton classes, was nothing special, and no one cared about its history or architecture. The college buildings where I went for my liberal arts courses were dingy and dilapidated. Houston Hall was a place many of the students went between classes, and it was an okay building.

We played pick-up basketball every afternoon. That was my

passion. One game in particular comes to mind. We were close to the end when one of my teammates got hurt and could not continue. It was up to me to choose his replacement. Marty Caplan, one of my best friends, appeared to be my first option, but I chose the only other one I had, a complete stranger who happened to be playing on our team for some unknown reason. Why did I do that? It was not premeditated in any way. I never thought about it. It was instinctive. The stranger was a better player than Marty and could help our team win. It was only a pick-up game, but I never liked to lose.

The same can't be said for my studies. When I was taking courses at Penn, grades were never important to me, as they never were in high school, either.

Playing basketball, however, brought out a different side of me. In that arena (or on the playgrounds), I would do anything to win. During sophomore year, my friend, Mike Singer, challenged John Canzano and John Cardeses to a best of three game series of 2-on-2 basketball, with me as his teammate. Each game went up to 15 baskets, and you had to win by two. John Canzano played varsity basketball, and Cardeses played junior varsity. Mike Singer was from New York and was a fine scoring guard. Me? I was tall, had some skills, and played with passion.

The games were exhausting. We split the first two and won a close third game. When Canzano went to varsity practice the next day, his teammates asked him what had happened with our challenge. When he told them he lost, they laughed him out of the gym. They had no idea that Mike and I were city boys who could actually play.

Early on in my freshman year, Dick Harter, the freshman coach, tracked me down and asked me to try out for the team. I went to one practice, which started at five p.m. I was commuting at the time, and when I showed up and had a look at the guys, I knew right away that I was not a better player than any of the scholarship people on the team. It made no sense to be there, so I never went back. Instead, I played pickup at the gym as much as I could.

There are no career positions for pickup basketball players. You just play. Maybe my love of doo-wop served me well in that environment, because when it's played right, basketball is terrifically musical, and when you're playing well, you really swing.

Summertime

MY FRESHMAN YEAR ENDED FINE with Bs and Cs, but I needed a summer job. Luckily, I was recruited to be a counselor at Green Lane, a Jewish overnight camp. Jerry Stein offered me $100 plus tips for the season, and I took it. Ernie Beck, a former All-American basketball player at Penn, was a counselor, too. He went on to play with the Philadelphia Warriors when they won an NBA championship in the mid-50s.

He and I were friendly. One time, before a nighttime activity, he asked if I wanted to play some ball. The first person to make three shots while the other missed won the game. I took seven out of the nine games we played. I made all his jump shots, plus I could shoot a two-hand set shot, which he couldn't. The next day, a 12-year-old challenged me to the same game and beat me two out of three. Big shot one day and humbled the next.

We played teams from the city and other camps once or twice a week. Pickles Kennedy, Bruce Drysdale, and four other top high school and college players came up one night. We lost by seven points. Ernie had 20 points, and I had 15. Sometimes I played well, and other times, not so much.

It was a fun summer. I liked the other counselors and even the kids. The one downer? I had no romance the entire time.

In the summer of my sophomore year, I worked at Camp Laurel Lake with lots of people from New York. I was the sole counselor for four kids. I received $175 plus tips and a $25 bonus for my overall good performance.

Bernie Kerzner was the head counselor. He was the basketball coach at Erasmus High School in New York and brought many of his players to camp to work and play. I think he was also Billy Cunningham's coach in high school. We used to play three or four games a week against other camps and colleges, which was a lot of fun both on and off the court.

My friend, Jerry Bernstein, found these job openings for both of us. At the end of camp, the owner declined to give either of us the $25 bonus he had promised. Jerry wrote him an inflammatory letter. The owner, who was a lawyer, refused to give Jerry the bonus and was angry at the tone of his letter. I sat down and wrote a letter, too. I spoke about how much I had enjoyed working at the camp. I asked him if he would reconsider my bonus, since I had tried to do everything I could to provide my campers with a worthwhile experience. Two weeks later, a check for $25 arrived in the mail.

With Friends Like These . . .

JERRY AND I PLAYED A LOT of basketball together. We talked sports non-stop. We cruised for girls. It seemed like we were good friends, but things can change.

An incident occurred one evening, which caused me to never to see him again.

We met at a deli for dinner in northeast Philadelphia. Jerry had leased a brand-new white Cadillac. The other cars in the lot, including mine, paled in comparison. We ate dinner and paid by separate checks before walking out to the parking lot. Just before reaching our cars, we heard a brash voice behind us. It was the owner, standing on the top step, who was speaking to Jerry. I was standing next to him.

"You stiffed my waitress," the owner said, "and you have done it before. Don't ever come into this restaurant again."

He meant me, too, in a simple case of guilt by association. I never took Jerry's calls and never saw him again. He passed a few years back.

Jerry and I had some good times together, but that incident shows how friendships can come and go pretty easily, especially when one of the parties violates the usual norms of good behavior.

Other times, what seems like a good thing at first might not turn out that way, and it's often a mystery as to why that happens. For example, in my senior year, my cousin Sheila introduced me to a tall, attractive, and sensual blond, whom I dated. She liked me. She told me her favorite song was "My Funny Valentine." Her name was Elaine Weisbart. She lived in northern Jersey. For some reason, I stopped seeing her.

I enjoyed other good friendships. Steve Goodman played jazz piano every day, and I loved listening to him. Steve was in Wharton and later was #1 in his class at Penn Law School. I went to see him at his office after his graduation, and he was very accommodating and a wonderful guy. Sadly, he recently passed.

Ben Lerner, who was in my freshman class, transferred to Brandeis University. He later attended Penn Law School and worked in the public defender's office before becoming a judge. He loved baseball, like me, and he played for many years in leagues around the city. His brother, Alan, was also a lawyer who taught at the law school. He was a great guy and a client of mine. He passed a few years ago.

Staying alive at 78 years old is not a given.

Say What?

I LIKED MY PUBLIC SPEAKING CLASS. One assignment required us to bring in an object and explain how it worked. All week long, I had no clue what I would do. Sunday night, just before class the next day, something kicked in. I went to class with a baseball and demonstrated how to throw a fastball, curve, and change-up. I got a rare A for that talk.

Another time, I had to present all the pros and cons of being in a fraternity. I started with the cons and did a good job, but the teacher said I should have started with the positives. I got a B for the course, which was great for me. That's because I was engaged. When I wasn't, I drifted, and bad things happened to my grades.

I had an outstanding European history teacher. She was an obvious lesbian to most of us, telegraphed by her dress and hair and her demeanor. The administration could see it, too, and she never was given the chance to deliver the main lecture for our class, although it was apparent to anyone that she was much more qualified than her male counterpart who gave the presentations. I was mesmerized by her knowledge and got an A in the final, the only one I got in four years.

In psychology class, I met a nice guy named Frederick Kramer, Who thought I might want to pledge his fraternity. He invited me to lunch at the frat house, where we ate baloney and mayonnaise sandwiches with pickles and potato chips. For a hungry college boy, what could be better? I showed no interest in pledging, however, and he never looked my way or talked to me again. It was nothing personal about him, but he took it that way.

There have been many people I've come across in my lifetime who have found me annoying or too intense or something else. You can't please everyone, though, so you may as well please yourself. In fact, there should be a song about that.

Marty, Malcolm, Billy and I were friends when we started our freshman year together. Using public transportation to the campus from our homes in the northeast section of the city was not an easy task. We formed a car pool, and each of us drove one week at a time. Those guys were all Central High graduates and academically proficient, as opposed to me, who made a habit of just getting by.

Marty graduated Phi Beta Kappa and became an actuary. Later, he moved out west to become the headmaster of a school. I applaud him for that. His father, Lou, and my father, Morris, were friends for many years. Lou was a nice man; I liked him.

Malcolm was a big guy with an olive complexion. I nicknamed him Newk, after Don Newcomb, the great Dodger pitcher. I saw a resemblance, and other people started calling him Newk, too, which he didn't particularly like. Malcolm and I lived in a large house on campus during our senior year. The majority of the Penn varsity basketball team lived there, too. John Wideman lived in the room next to me. He became a highly acclaimed author. Malcolm went to Penn Law School and unfortunately has passed away.

My friend, Mike Braude, and I had a dinner partnership in that house. He cooked, and I cleaned up. My parents gave me an allowance of $20 a week, which meant we ate a lot of spaghetti.

Billy Richman was in our car pool. He was a chemistry major and later earned his doctorate at Penn. Billy would always describe his sexual escapades with various women. I was a little envious, I must admit.

One day, we came to Bill's home to pick him up, and he wasn't ready. This happened many times. Finally, one day when I was driving, I left without him. He was angry when he saw me later that day, but he wasn't late anymore.

I value all of my friends from those days, even the ones I never saw again.

The 12th of Never

RELATIONSHIPS ARE A CORNERSTONE of going to college. I had many nice classmates at Penn, and still keep up with a few of them. In fact, a few guys really helped me in my business. The friends I made were always more important to me than the subject matter of any of my classes. Unfortunately, I guess, I never had enough friends. My social life at Penn, throughout my four years there, was on a par with my academic performance. Dismal.

I asked a young female student to go out with me, someone I knew from our childhood neighborhood. I knew she was a very good math student when I asked her out, and when she said yes, I thought, oh goody!

It was a beautiful spring evening when we drove to a spot on East River Drive. It was very romantic there, full of many people parked in their cars, like us. We got out of the car and found a secluded spot. We spoke for a while.

Then I got up the courage to make my move. I put my arm around her. That went well. Not first base. Ball Three, young man. I leaned in to kiss her and she pulled away. I was stunned. What had I done wrong? Did my arm hold her too hard or too loose? No. She said kissing me would be like kissing her brother. She also told me she liked olive-skinned boys and had a crush on a fellow classmate, named Joel. If you don't want to be kissed by a guy, I thought, why would you go out with him? I didn't get it. She was so good at math and so academically smart. How did this happen?

I thought back on other failed ventures I'd had with women. I flashed back on the time when I missed seeing the great Oscar Robertson play in the Palestra because I took a girl to a boring wedding reception. When I wanted to go to my senior prom—God knows why—my father allowed me to drive his Oldsmobile 88. He loved that car and was sure I would get in an accident.

Her name was Diane Weisberg. Her father was a friend of my mother from Scranton. They lived in Mount Airy. I asked her to be my date for the prom. Her parents were religious Jews. The prom was on a Friday night. I thought this would present a major problem, but they let her go. After the prom, we headed to the first of a few after-parties, but Diane fell asleep on the ride to the first one. She never woke up until I got her home. She had big breasts, and I had been hoping for some action, but I never received anything except a sleepy kiss good night.

In my junior year, I dated a girl named Sharon Kaplan. I had never dated a girl more than three times. After three dates, you had to get somewhere on the base paths or call it a day. I never did, and for good reason. I was boring. They were boring. Sharon was going to Temple University to become an elementary school teacher. She had dark hair and dark eyes. We would go out to a movie, or go bowling, or to a Temple football game. Then we would head back to her home on Sharpnack Street in Mount Airy, where we would go down to the basement and make out. She only got into it if I played a special Johnny Mathis song, "The Twelfth of Never."

When it came to dating, it was always the 12th of never. After seven or eight dates, I wanted her to remove her sweater and show me her breasts so I could see them, fondle them, and caress them.

"I am saving them for my husband."

That was her response, one that still haunts me today. Not her virginity! Her breasts! She was saving her breasts for . . . never mind. It was more pain and humiliation from yet one more woman. This rejection was becoming part of my DNA.

I continued to date Sharon. Schmuck! A week later I called and could not get her on the phone. I always called and planned some venue for our Saturday date. Not this time. Later, I found out she went to Rutgers for the weekend with a guy who was a student there. I exploded in a fit of rage and jealousy. I wrote her a break up letter, whaling my frustration at her in words.

She must have shown that letter to every friend or person she knew at the time, because it came back to haunt me many years later. I met a woman and told her my name.

"Oh, you're the guy with the letter, right?"

I was stunned. Sharon, wherever you are, I hope you got married and your husband had a chance to enjoy seeing and fondling your breasts.

Eventually, I realized that part of my problem was the fact that I was dating only Jewish women. In high school, most of my female classmates were gentile. Some were very attractive, and I spoke to them in an easy and effective manner. Why didn't I ask them out when I had the chance?

It's too late now. That's life—just another opportunity gained and another one missed, as well.

In the Family Footsteps

I MAJORED IN INSURANCE AT PENN. Both my father and grandfather, Sam, were in the insurance business. He had a large extended family. He tried to sell insurance to all of them. His brother, David, who spelled his last name Krausan, was financially successful, as were his sons, who attended Germantown Academy, a prestigious private school, where my uncle served on the board.

He called my father after learning of my basketball background to see if I had any interest in a scholarship to attend that school. Our family had limited contact with that side of the family, and I had no interest in attending a school like that.

My grandfather set up shop in a Horn & Hardart's to solicit customers. Sam would sell these unsuspecting people property, casualty, disability, and life insurance. Money was tight back then, so he would buy a roll and make himself a ketchup sandwich, which he made last most of the day while he hustled his business.

His wife, my grandmother, Ida, had a heart of gold. She belonged to all the Jewish charity groups. The two of them fought in Yiddish, which none of us could understand. However, the tone and loud pitch of their arguments told us all we needed to know.

Whenever I played cards with my grandfather, he tried to cheat if he started losing. He would laugh when I caught him, which I often did. He was an Orthodox Jew, and I went to synagogue with him a few times. As that tradition dictated, women sat in a separate balcony from the men, rendering them second-class citizens. I sat there with my mother sometimes.

After graduating from college, my father worked in a liquor store and then worked at the William Penn Annex at Ninth and Market. I visited him there once and was startled to see that there was a window with bars between us. It was like he was in jail. He must have felt that way, too. His nervous breakdown, which caused him to spend a week in a mental hospital, must have been, at least in part, a reaction to all of that.

Sometime during the 1950-1951 school year, my father borrowed money from my Aunt Sadie to help him go full-time into the insurance business. His cousin, Ruby Cardonick, lived on Levick Street. He told everyone on his block to buy insurance from his cousin, Morrie. Many of them did. This was a genuine act of kindness and really helped my father launch his business.

Ruby had two sons, Larry and Sheldon. Larry was an all-state football player at Olney High School. Few linemen from city schools became all-state players, because most of them were big, tough kids from coal mining towns in central and western Pennsylvania. Larry got a full ride to Temple University. One night, he intercepted a pass and ran the ball into the end zone for a touchdown. His mother, Gert, was in the bathroom at the time and missed it. Too bad! At five foot nine and 205 pounds, Larry was a mean athlete and ended up playing professionally in Canada. If he had been bigger, especially with his talent and rare warrior demeanor, he would have been an outstanding pro in the NFL.

Sheldon, my other cousin, was a terrific guy and a very good basketball player. We won a championship together in an over-40 league in 1994. Sheldon contracted ALS about 10 years ago and has since passed. I miss him.

The Insurance Gods

A REQUIREMENT FOR GRADUATING the insurance program was passing a comprehensive test with at least a 70, which was not automatic for me. The other rule was that everyone had to write a thesis, which required a great deal of time and research.

I got a 76 on the exam and received a C on my thesis, which was about aviation insurance. I spent hours doing research at the INA building. INA later changed their name to Cigna, the letters INA are still chiseled in the stone where the building stands today.

By the second half of my junior year, I had saved enough money to live on campus. My roommate, who shared the cost 50/50, was an Irish man from Boston by the name of Jim Maloney. He had come back to Penn to take one course in casualty insurance with H. Wayne Snyder. He had needed a 70 to pass the course and finished with a 69. He went to Professor Snyder to plead his case. Snyder was a staunch Republican from the state of Washington. He hated Franklin Roosevelt and The New Deal. Jim Maloney lost his appeal and was placed in my class.

Snyder was a fine teacher but a real hard-ass who took no prisoners. He later became the chairman of the insurance department at Temple University.

Once, when there was a huge snowstorm, many people did not go to class. Unfortunately for me, I was one of them. Snyder put three questions on the next test that no one who missed class that day could have answered. No chance! He told people in the class

131

that those questions would be on the test. He also said that if anyone who had not been in class that day got the answers from someone who had, that they would automatically fail the course.

No one said a word. I lost 15 points as soon as the test began. I had no clue what the answers were or where the information even came from. Snyder took no prisoners; that's for sure. I snuck out of the class with a D. Maloney passed, too. We can thank the insurance gods for that.

Get Me Outa Here!

I WAS READY TO FINISH THE ACADEMIC LIFE. During my four years at Penn, I had drifted from feeling lost in my own head to suffering from bouts of depression and melancholia. I was never specifically anxious about grades, because I only cared about passing. I had no goal of attending graduate school. My plan was to go into the insurance business, which seemed simple enough, until it wasn't.

I had some fun at Penn, especially at football games and watching Big Five basketball games at the Palestra, when Penn faced other iconic Philadelphia universities—St. Joseph's, Lasalle, Temple, and Villanova. I made some nice friends at those events.

C. Douglas Dillon, the Unites States Secretary of the Treasury, gave the commencement address at graduation. It was dreadful. What a disappointing day to end my four years, but it wasn't such a big deal, because I was already anxious to move on with my life.

Fortunately, I left Penn with one indelible memory from my junior year, when Ayn Rand came to speak. Too bad she wasn't our commencement speaker! She was a strong believer in the ability of an individual to shape his or her own life and success. This was all about the alpha male and female.

I became inspired to read her books. *Fountain Head* was my initiation, and they made a movie based on the book. I believe Rand's parents were Communists. When she gave her talk, she received a lot of backlash from the students. Ed Snyder, the future owner of the Philadelphia Flyers hockey team, became one of her disciples. Paul Ryan, Speaker of the House of Representatives, was a devotee, as well.

I never joined any type of admiration society, but her philosophy is not without merit. Where her philosophy is flawed and becomes subject to conjecture is when you consider that not everyone has the capacity or the opportunity to reach the top. Not everyone can realize that pinnacle. Role players are necessary, in sports and in life. There are worker bees and drones. That said, digging into yourself to find your best and going to places you had previously been afraid to go is something to live for, and I like to think I've done some of that in my life.

RICHARD G. KRASSEN

Expanding My Horizons

THE SUMMER OF 1962 proved quite eventful. I wanted to travel the country and needed someone to share the expenses and be a good companion. My immediate friends weren't available and I was hesitant to ask anyone I didn't know very well.

Luckily, my Aunt Bea helped to solve the problem. She lived in Chevy Chase, Maryland with my Uncle Jack, an economist with a PhD. Aunt Bea knew someone whose son had just graduated from Haverford College. He played football, but he was not that big, so I figured we could both fit inside his car. He agreed to drive his Pontiac, and we split all the expenses. It sure seemed fair to me.

We decided to camp at sites all over the country. We bought supplies to cook and eat, purchased a tent, and stocked up at the super market on cereal and other staples. I took along a book with the names, addresses, and phone number of fellow Penn graduates who lived all across the country.

The first day was nice, and we drove all the way to Shaker Heights, Ohio. Bob Jenks, my fellow traveler, had a friend and classmate who lived there, and his family served us a wonderful meal and provided comfortable mattresses for us to sleep on after our long drive. It was a great start. Our host's mother was very nice and said something revealing, which I still remember.

"I always let my husband feel like he is the boss, even though in many cases I get my way."

What a brilliant woman.

Bob and I were on the road for ten weeks. On many days, we found campsites and enjoyed being outdoors. It rained sometimes, but we had no problems with the elements.

Our most significant stop was the singular day and night we spent in the city of Chicago. That 24 hours still glistens in my memory. We had barely arrived when we walked by a strip club, where a man was flipping a silver dollar, trying to get our attention along with all the others passing by.

"Anyone want a date with one of the girls?"

I was a virgin and wanted to get laid. Bob was experienced. He had been with an older woman in college who had allowed him to drive her car. What a stud. I was still green enough to be envious and overly needy, too.

I soon discovered there was a price to pay for my hunger. After acknowledging to the guy that wanted a date, I went with him on a city bus to an apartment house on what someone referred to as the "bad side of town." As soon as we got upstairs, he told me to give him my watch, my ring, and ten dollars. He left me sitting on a beat-up couch while he entered a doorway, telling me the woman would be out shortly. I waited, wondering what she would be like and how I would fare with her. My imagination was running as wild as my heartbeat. I don't know how much time passed while I waited in anticipation, but whoever she was she never came out. Neither did that guy. I ended up losing the money, my watch, and my college ring, the one my parents had purchased for me right after graduation, which I proudly wore on our trip across the States. Big mistake.

One day, city police in Chicago might do an autopsy on some John Doe and will find my ring. Maybe they did already, and someone is wearing it around, advertising the Class of 1962. Pre-Trump, by the way. Someone must have it. Somewhere. Enjoy it. With my cumulative average, I shouldn't have been allowed to wear it anyway. I told my mother and father I left it in a washroom in Chicago when I removed it to wash my hands. I can still hear my mother yelling at me from her grave.

I reported the incident to the police, who were amused but sympathetic. They saw how pathetic I was, a kid so wet behind the ears. One officer told me that a stiff dick has no conscience. He also said something that saved our trip.

"If you leave your car overnight with everything in view it will be gone in the morning, for sure."

Amazingly, he allowed Bob and me to park in a secured police parking lot. We had to be out by six a.m., so we set an alarm and were on our way right on time.

That was my sole experience in the Windy City until recently. My granddaughter, Sydney, is a student at the University of Wisconsin. My wife, Carole, and I flew out to Chicago on a stopover to see her. My old friend, Walter Brown, and his wife, Selma, met us at the airport. We stayed with them in Chicago before taking a bus to Madison to attend Sydney's graduation.

The boat ride on Chicago's main river to see the wonderful architecture was quite spectacular, but it could not erase the memory of my first trip to that great city. What was I thinking, that the woman would come out of her lair, wearing my ring and watch, with my ten-dollar bill in her bra, inviting me to come with her for the ride of my life? Onward and upward was my only option.

The Grand Canyon became our next prime destination. Bob decided we should walk down the trail from the top slope to the base at the Colorado River. We had some water, but soon found out it was not enough. Summertime in Arizona is stifling, especially in the desert. Some people were descending the canyon on donkeys. Going down all that way was not a terrible problem, even though we were exhausted and dehydrated when we got there. We found water in a cabin and slept like babies.

Starting back, we found out pretty soon what we were up against. It seemed like it got dark very fast, long before we were near the top, which presented a big problem. It was getting difficult to see, and we had no flashlight. Big mistake. The temperature had already dropped about 40 degrees and was continuing to fall.

Bob was in much better shape than I. For me, the whole march was grueling. Okay, that was an understatement. I was exhausted. Each of my legs seemed to weigh a ton. That's not an exaggeration. They felt so heavy, I thought I was going to fall off a cliff on my left or into a ravine on my right. Either way, it was all I could do to put one foot in front of the other and make it back to the top. Barely.

As soon as we got back to the tent, I hit the hay and slept deeply until the next morning. When I awoke, my head was totally clear. It has not been since. Maybe I should go back and redo my adventure. Then again, maybe at age 78, I shouldn't.

Yellowstone was our next memorable site. The geysers were splendid. We met a man while camping there who appeared at first to be friendly. We visited him in his tent. I was tired and went back to our tent to sleep. Bob told me in the morning that the man showed him pornographic pictures and asked him to sleep inside his tent. It never happened. I guess the guy stalked campsites looking for young male prey, and we certainly qualified.

From there, we continued north until we reached Crater Lake in Oregon. The pure blue color of that water was beautiful. I can still see that lake in my mind, and the vision of it is still so peaceful.

Our next stop was in Seattle, where we headed straight for the iconic space needle. After that, we headed for Vancouver, Canada.

Bob and I wasted no time making our way to San Francisco and across the bay to the campus at Cal/Berkley. We met some students there at a party, and Bob and I got separated and slept in different rooms. One guy had a mattress for me. Big mistake. He also had pills of every color and size on his bureau. In the middle of the night, he started screaming, waking me and everyone else on the floor.

Along the coastal highway to Los Angeles, we hooked up with a Penn coed who cooked us a nice dinner. We didn't stay long, as we were itching to drive north and escape the heat.

We headed straight out of there and drove south to San Diego. For some reason, we couldn't find a cheap hotel or camping spot, so we slept on the beach. At least we tried. I slept fitfully, fearing we would be attacked by a gang of surfers or a school of sharks, on the prowl for horny college graduates.

Our loop around the country then took us on a long ride south to Texas, where something tragic was thankfully avoided. Driving down the highway one night, a man appeared in our headlights. Bob was driving, which he did most of the time. In this case, since the car was his, too, he was the de facto alpha male. That meant it was his call whether we stopped or not. The man was walking backwards on a very hot patch of blacktop. We barely avoided hitting him and stopped to pick him up. He was quite inebriated and was going on and on about how he was a former major league baseball player for the St. Louis Browns.

We had no reason to believe him or think he was full of it. So with nothing seemingly better to do, we drove him to see his daughter, who lived in southern Texas. It was about 200 miles out of our way, but he was amiable enough and full of stories, so we drove into the night until we could drop him off at his daughter's place. She was so glad to greet her father. She hadn't seen him in some time. That was our good deed for a fellow ballplayer.

We visited the Alamo in San Antonio. Standing there, imagining the history of that place, I kept thinking that must have been some battle, and what would have become of Texas and the United States if it had turned out a different way?

New Orleans was even hotter and more humid. We headed to the beach, where we saw a beautiful, young, tall woman walking with a short, unattractive man with black, horn-rimmed glasses.

"Why is this beautiful young woman with this old unattractive man?" Bob said.

I never answered him at the time, but I will now. She was probably with him because of symbiosis, when creatures of different species come together for mutually beneficial reasons. This young and beautiful female creature was together with an older, much less attractive creature because he was undoubtedly rich and probably her boss. I think they both got something out of the relationship. He had leverage and got what he wanted from her, while she was seeking something more in life and was getting what she needed—at least temporarily—from him. We saw many young, beautiful women in New Orleans during our few days there, and I still wonder how many of them had similar arrangements.

In the French Quarter, we came across an African American man slumped over but still on his feet as he attempted to cross the street. He was old and seemed disabled. My instinct led me to run to his side to help him across this wide, busy street. I wanted him to be safe. Another African American man looked incredulously at me, as if he couldn't believe a young, white man would help an older black man with anything. This was 1962, so my action must have stood out, especially in the south.

I loved the music in New Orleans and always hope to return.

The rest of the trip was blur, and still is, even today.

We went back to Bob's home, and I met his lovely mother. Bob thought of his father as an economic failure, which I thought was unfortunate. Bob also considered me to be inept, and he made that known to me, especially through his temper, which could flare up pretty badly on occasion.

Ten weeks with the same person—24 hours a day, much of it in the confines of a car, was tough on both of us. By the time we were done, we had both had enough. A month after returning home, I sent Bob a short story about our trip, which he really liked. That made me feel better about him and the trip I came to treasure, and still do. The best part was that I helped make that trip happen.

Rejected!

AFTER GRADUATION, I APPLIED FOR EMPLOYMENT at several companies. One in particular led me to believe that they didn't like graduates from Ivy League schools. I had a good interview, nonetheless.

On the application, they asked my religious affiliation. I put Jewish. The interviewer read my application with me in the room. He winked at me. I didn't know why.

Shortly thereafter, I received a terse rejection letter. Was it because I was Jewish? Maybe. I will never know, but in 1962, in Philadelphia, I don't know if this should have come as a surprise.

Joining the Air Force

I JOINED A MEDICAL SUPPORT UNIT of the Air Force reserves in 1963 after signing up at a recruitment office on Courtland Street. Entering the military was not a voluntary choice like it is now, but luckily, I was able to choose which specific branch I entered. The Reserves seemed best and a medic unit sounded appealing.

Just after New Year's, I flew with my friend, Marty, to San Antonio, Texas, for six weeks of basic training. It was pitch dark each morning when we woke at five. Some days were cold and some were warm, so we never knew what type of weather we'd be facing, but our assigned clothing never changed. We were issued a big, blue, heavy overcoat, which was very hard to pack.

We were allowed to sleep in on Sundays, which we all enjoyed. Still, all of that bright and early physical conditioning got me into better shape than I'd ever been in.

We bunked four to a room. Pat, from South Philadelphia, was my bunkmate. One of the other fellas, who loved to talk politics, was from North Carolina, and the fourth came from Oklahoma. Although he made it clear that he did not like Jews, for some reason he told me that I was a good Jew, whatever that means.

Kyle Acre was in our unit. He spent six weeks marching behind me, stepping on my heels, just to remind me that he didn't like me. He had flunked out of college in his freshman year, and apparently the years he spent growing up in Georgia hadn't done anything to make him any smarter.

They gave us 10 articles on military procedures, which we were supposed to memorize. Twice, when I was given one to recall and recite, I froze. They gave out punishment each time you screwed up. I earned more than my share.

Overall, it was not a bad experience. We had no severe marches to endure in rainstorms. The food was not great, but edible. We played some touch football; I was good at that. Thankfully, they never issued rifles or other weapons, which I found good.

I looked forward to attending the military tech school for ten weeks, which was located at Gunter Air Force base in Montgomery, Alabama. They provided courses in anatomy, medicine, and surgery, and I've never forgotten some of what I learned there.

Sometimes on weekends, two other airmen and I would drive to the University of Alabama. I knew a student there whose name was Newman, and I brought him a carton of cigarettes. He let me sleep at his apartment, which worked out well.

At the end of that sequence, I returned home. I had to go back to my reserve unit one weekend a month for the next five-and-a-half years, to fulfill my obligation. To keep us prepared for active duty at any time, we also did a two-week refresher stint each year.

Hello, My Name Is Mr. Krassen

WITH NO FULL-TIME JOB AVAILABLE, I signed up to substitute teach in District 5 of the City of Philadelphia public school system. I found plenty of work right away in four junior high schools: Wanamaker, Stetson, Penn Treaty, and Jones. I was young and not prepared for the daily torture.

Every morning I received a phone call, telling me which school to report to and what course I would be teaching, or at least trying to, however I could manage. In all honesty, there was very little teaching going on in those classrooms. The kids knew I had no leverage, so they constantly acted up. On one occasion, a class broke out in laughter when someone went to the board and erased the K-R and E-N from my last name, leaving a big A-S-S displayed on the blackboard.

I earned $23 a day, but I was still living at home and banking the money. However, it was not enough to buy a car, even in 1963. I asked my father to help me purchase a new one, because my 1953 Chevy was in pretty bad shape by then. I had my eye on a black Pontiac Tempest convertible.

We went to the dealer on Bustleton Avenue and negotiated a good price. Back in those days, you had to order a car, which I hated doing, because that meant you had to wait for it to come in. Today, you can check an app, order what you want, and pick it up. The cars are made much better now, too. Foreign competition has been a big help in that regard.

American car companies projected that a car they produced could run for 50,000 miles before needing any type of major repair.

Back then, the formula was simple. A man walked into a showroom and bought a Chevy. That meant taking out a bank note for four years, but cars were not that expensive. In fact, most people I knew paid off their loan, and as soon as they made their last installment, they went back to the same dealer and bought a new car.

For the American automobile industry, this was certainly a beautiful business model. All the salesmen kept a book of customer records, so with that history available in the file cabinets, they could predict sales for most every month. Plus, you always had the walk-ins, like us.

By 1964, we not only had The Beatles and the British invasion; this was also the dawn of the Japanese car invasion. For the most part, the cars had little style, but they were reliable enough to run well for up to 100,000 miles. Do the math.

They told us the car we ordered would take four to six weeks to arrive. Spring was already in full bloom, and I wanted to enjoy my new ride with the top down. After six weeks had passed, we called every two or three days, but by then my appetite for that car had surely waned. I finally told my father I didn't want the car.

Thankfully, we got our deposit back. A week later, the dealership called to announce that the car had arrived. They asked if we wanted it, but I said no.

I never regretted it. It turns out I wasn't a convertible guy, after all. I became more of a safe, classic, four-door-sedan type of guy. Now, I drive a 2010 Honda Accord. That's me. Solid. Reliable. Not high maintenance or high end.

The '53 Chevy and I stayed together a little while longer, and that felt fine for the time being. I enjoyed driving around on my own sometimes, making up ideas for what I might try teaching the children in school. Since it was difficult getting through to them sometimes, I quite enjoyed the success I had sharing some original aphorisms I wrote especially for them.

Mathematics is a mental discipline in problem solving.
Maybe the world needs a crash course in math.

That got 'em thinking, for a few minutes at least.

In man's quest for knowledge and pleasure,
His greatest hope is in the utilization of his senses.

As soon as I explained what this meant, many of the kids related to it.

Most successful people learn early in life to distinguish between what they should *do and what they* have *to do.*

Naturally, lots of my students related to this concept, as they saw it in action each and every day in the hallways and classrooms of our school.

Susan

I MET SOMEONE. She liked me. I liked her. What could be better than that?

Susan lived five blocks from my home. In 1963, people who got married were likely to live within 20 blocks of each other, and Susan and I were no different. I had little idea, however, what I was about to enter into that summer, and what a major turning point in my life was about to happen.

My mother, Vera—the same one who locked me out of the house when I was a little boy—played cards with a woman named Pauline. Beware the Perils of Pauline! She often spoke of her daughter, Susan, an only child, who grew up on Unruh Street, just east of Bustleton Avenue. I could walk there easily from my house.

Susan played piano and received a scholarship to study voice at the Boston University School of Fine and Applied Arts. Upon graduating, her professors told her she was not good enough to be a successful opera singer and advised her to become a music teacher. Susan and her parents embraced this advice, and she taught music in the West Boylston school district in Massachusetts.

Pauline had a master's degree and taught special education in the Philadelphia public school system. Adolph, Susan's father, was a graduate of Fordham Law School.

Susan was fairly tall and slim, and I found her very attractive. She was a brunette, and I loved brunettes: Ava Gardner, Heddy Lamar, Elizabeth Taylor. Susan was not exactly all that, but she was close enough for me. After all, I was no Clark Gable or Errol Flynn, so maybe the two of us would be a good match.

I called her up when she came back home to see her parents. Pauline told my mother that Susan was engaged to a man named Richard Cohn, a musician who wanted his life to revolve around music. His father was a successful businessman with a company called Burlington, but Richard wanted no part of that.

Pauline's father, who lived in New York City, had a successful dry-cleaning business, mainly because he did all the clothes for Broadway stars. When Pauline married Adolph, she thought he would become a financial success as a lawyer, but it didn't work out that way.

He had a beautiful office in New York City, but his personality was incompatible with getting clients. His mother was a strict German who dominated her husband, who worked as a barber. She also had a debilitating effect on Adolph, who was quite proper and had trouble taking the initiative. Pauline reminded him of that every now and then, and even did the same with Susan. The Perils of Pauline, remember? Susan's father was a very nice man. He wound up working at the Veterans Administration in Philadelphia, which is why the whole family moved here.

Bea Kravitz, a friend of my mother, had tickets to the Robin Hood Dell in the park. This was a great classical music work, and Susan and I were excited to have such good seats up front. Wow, I was so attracted to her, I had a hard time focusing on the music. I think she liked me, too.

Soon after Susan returned to Massachusetts, Pauline went up there and convinced her daughter to break off her engagement. Her selling point was that Richard would not make a good living as a musician; therefore, what kind of husband could he be? Susan bought it, which was possibly a mistake on her part. The fact that I was a Wharton graduate, like the Donald, must have been a point in my favor. Pauline assumed I was destined to become a financial success, which meant I should also be good husband material. Ha. Just goes to show that first impressions can be tricky.

Susan and I saw each other as much as possible that summer. I had to go away for my required two-week stint in the Air Force Reserve. The plane was leaving at 3:30 in the morning. My friend, Marty, and his fiancé were driving me to Willow Grove early that morning. Susan said she wanted to see me off, too, which was quite something for me. I felt like here was someone I could trust to stick by me. At 23 years old, I didn't know much. I like to think I'm a little smarter now.

Susan and I continued our long-distance dating throughout the fall. She taught music at Neshaminy. She loved the kids and was the chorus leader. They put on a wonderful Christmas show. The suburban schools in Pennsylvania paid their teachers poorly but the Philadelphia school district paid better. Susan planned to transfer here for the following year, which turned out to be a real mistake.

In December, I bought an engagement ring at Kelmer's Jewelers. Leon Oram was the salesman; I still remember him and his bright red hair.

I spent the year substitute teaching and selling insurance, which is a dynamite combination, especially if you like pain and feeling constant rejection.

Like my father and grandfather, I was licensed to sell all kinds of insurance. I started selling auto to people between 18 and 25. The Hartford had very competitive rates for people in this class, and I built up a nice book of business. I also sold tenant and homeowner's policies to young people getting married and moving into their first home.

The *Jewish Exponent* announced local engagements each week, and I scoured the paper for leads I could cold call while the iron was hot. I sold term life insurance to my young married friends who had little money to spend.

Overall, I must say this created a depressing existence for me. Little did I know at the time that it would get worse—way worse.

We got married on August 16, 1964, at Temple Shalom on Large Street in Oxford Circle. I was Bar Mitzvah'ed there. Between all of the planning and everyone having an opinion about this and that, I felt like I was being swept up in big wave and carried out to sea. The horizon seemed so far away, and I had a lot of apprehension about what I was getting into. At the same time, I was excited for this new chapter in my life.

Big changes are funny. Like an iceberg, you only see one seventh of it on the surface. The rest is hidden until you start sinking and crashing into it. I ended up doing a lot of crashing.

We went to Puerto Rico for our honeymoon. The hotel and resort were beautiful. When we returned to Philly, we started a whole new life by signing a lease to live at the Welsh Revere duplex apartments in the northeastern part of the city. The rent was $75 a month, plus utilities, and included a garage. What could go wrong?

The first thing that tipped me off to what was coming was when I realized that Susan had become my official partner. By virtue of the marriage contract we signed and the vows we took, we were now joined at the hip. Somehow, I had a gut feeling that this was not a terribly good idea, especially in the long run.

What were my options? A medical operation to become "disjointed" would have been very expensive and quite risky. In our case, the procedure would end up being performed by lawyers instead of surgeons.

In the meantime, I tried to keep a positive outlook, and whenever I could I turned my attention to my first love—sports. Susan's parents had no interest in ballgames of any kind. I don't think her father had ever even watched a ball game in his entire life. They had a television in their basement but rarely watched it. Instead, they read books, magazines, and journals and listened to classical music.

At first, Susan seemed indifferent to any of this.

I put on the radio to listen to the Phillies whenever I could. They were playing great baseball in 1964, with Dick Allen, Johnny Callison, Jim Bunning, and Chris Short. This was a team that had lost 23 straight games in 1961. I heard the win that broke that streak. They managed a 9-3 win in the second game of a Sunday doubleheader. John Buzzard was our starting pitcher; I cheered him on all the way.

The Phils were leading the league when we came back from our honeymoon in August. Susan informed me that she did not like listening to the Phillies game on the radio. We had a small apartment, so this left us few options. I found a way to listen every night through the month of September, when they had a six-and-a-half game lead with only twelve games to play.

Every day, the newspaper printed a big number on the front page, indicating how many games the Phillies needed to clinch the pennant. The temperature outside was hot that summer, and over the last two weeks, it felt like the entire city melted down as the Phillies failed to win another game, blew their lead, and wasted the whole season in one fell swoop.

Finally, the paper just stopped saying a word about it. I remember every single game we lost during that awful, agonizing, ten-game stretch. Our pitching was shot. Our bullpen could not hold a lead to save their life. Cincinnati, St. Louis, and the Braves beat up on us in succession—at home! The Cardinals eventually won the pennant on the final day of the season. They won the World Series, too, as if that was a consolation. No chance.

The player who stood out for me during that debacle was Johnny Callison. I loved that guy. On the last week of the season, he came down with an awful flu with a high fever. He played against the Cardinals anyway. When he drew a walk and trotted slowly down to first base, he was shaking. Only pitchers were allowed to wear jackets back then, and I think now, too. Somehow, Bill White, the first baseman, helped Johnny on with his jacket. It was the greatest act of sportsmanship I have ever seen. These two teams were battling for a pennant!

White later played for the Phillies and became a sports commentator on local television in Philadelphia. I wish I could've seen Johnny one more time before he died. We got him in a trade with the Chicago White Sox for Gene Freese. Great trade. Bunning from Detroit for Don Demeter was a great one, too.

Meanwhile, Susan started teaching music at Harding Junior High. This was much different from what she had grown used to, teaching younger kids in a suburb of Boston.

The discipline problem in Philadelphia junior high schools was apparent from the beginning. Mr. Scott, the principal, was told that I was a per diem substitute. He needed a gym teacher, and I was fine with that. I worked every day with a fellow teacher. Ira "The Large" Harge, a genuinely nice guy, was doing his student teaching after having attended The University of New Mexico.

Meanwhile, he had been drafted by the 76ers. He was definitely big enough—hence the nickname "Large," but he wasn't athletic enough to play at the NBA level. It was a good idea for him to pursue a career in teaching, and I'll bet he became quite good at it.

Things moved along fine at school, until one morning when Susan showed up at the gym to let me know she was cutting short her teaching day and going home. This was strange and totally unlike her. I figured she must have the flu, but she wasn't sick at all. I thought it had to be the flu. What did I know? Nothing. She was pregnant! Oh boy, I was not prepared for that kind of news.

I also wasn't expecting the school to hire a real gym teacher in the middle of the school year, but they did, and I was out of a job. Luckily, that didn't last long at all, because an English teacher announced she was pregnant and taking leave. I was asked to be her replacement. I worked there for the rest of the school year, till the end of June.

Maybe there was something in the water fountains at school, with two pregnancies occurring in such a short time.

One of my most memorable students at Harding Junior High was a young man named Thurman Bryson. He had attention deficit disorder and could not help becoming disruptive in class, which presented a problem for me and the other students, too.

One day, I kept him after school as a form of punishment. When

I went to the corner closet to get something, Thurman thought this was his chance to bolt. He made a break for the door. I heard him coming and not accidentally put my right forearm out to stop his motion. He hit my arm and fell to the floor. He wasn't hurt and sat back down. Soon enough, it was time to go home. I didn't think too much of it, because Thurman really liked me and had given me a small snapshot of himself. I thought we were cool and that he understood that I had to stop him.

Boy was I mistaken! The next day, a few children told me that Thurman's father was looking for me and that he had a gun. For reasons I cannot explain, I was not scared. I would be now, but back then, I just didn't see my situation as threatening.

Thurman's father never showed up, and the incident receded in my mind until it became another faded memory.

Around the same time, Mr. Scott made me a long-term substitute. I was on salary and got paid for sick days and holidays. What could be better? Most other things of course, but I was glad to have the security and a reason to stay focused.

I went to Temple University in the summer of 1962 after I graduated from Penn and took six teaching credits. I got an A in one course, which was my first one! I had never even come close to getting an A before. I passed the National Teachers exam and was hedging my bets on that career. Selling insurance on pure commission was dicey. Economic storm clouds were forming in the United States, but I never saw them coming. I was too busy teaching, preparing for my classes, and figuring out what becoming a father was going to mean for me.

Fatherhood

JOSH WAS BORN IN JUNE 1965, less than 10 months after Susan and I got married. Birth control? Nobody talked about that at the playground playing basketball. According to my sister, when Adolph and Pauline, Susan's parents, visited my parents' home they had a few choice words for my folks.

"Your son, Richard, is a dog for getting our daughter pregnant so soon after the wedding."

I'm sure they weren't joking. He obviously wasn't planned, but there were no regrets. Ever. Josh was a joy. He brought great pleasure to Susan and me, as well as to her parents and mine. I had loved the name Josh for a long time, so it's no wonder that we chose it for our first-born son. Way back, at Camp Kittatiny, one of the head counselors had a son named Josh. In 1965 it was not a very popular name, but that has surely changed.

We had a one-bedroom apartment, but when Josh was born, he and his crib were in the living room, so it was time to move.

Becoming a father was rough for me. I was only 25 years old and felt totally unprepared to have a child. Later that summer, I went to a Phillies-Cardinal doubleheader with some old friends. The Phillies won both, beating Bob Gibson in the opener. I was glad to have those activities with the guys, because I found it rough to find real satisfaction at home as a new husband and father.

One crisp winter day, while wheeling Josh in his carriage, this became clear for me.

What just happened?

I was definitely *not* ready for this responsibility or change in my lifestyle. First, a wife in 1964, and then a child less than one year later. Life was moving too fast. I began teaching in District 8 in the fall of 1964, which was a little better than District 5, where I had previously worked. It was closer to home, and the kids were better behaved, which meant I could spend less time enforcing discipline and more time actually teaching.

In October, I left for two weeks of Air Force reserve duty at Willow Grove. I was assigned to a motor pool, which meant no more work as a medic. They had disbanded the unit for reasons they never explained. On my first Saturday when I got there, another fellow and I couldn't find our unit. We decided to go home. That was not a smart move. We almost got court-martialed for going AWOL. Instead, we were disciplined with an Article 15, which meant we had to spend the next two weeks scrubbing toilets.

I was asked to drive a ton-and-a-half truck across the street to pick up some mechanical parts. I wasn't used to driving a truck with so much overhead. As I pulled in, I misjudged the height above me. The truck got stuck, and down came a multitude of light bulbs. The sergeant had to come over and get the truck separated from the wooden roof. He was really upset and never let me drive again during my entire two-week stint.

It was amazing how many things I could screw up.

In August, we flew on a C-119, a "flying boxcar," to Scott Air Force base in St. Louis. It was quite hot there. Each of us carried a parachute on our backs, which could be implemented if necessary. I was worried the entire time that I would have to jump. Unfortunately, it was a long ride, which allowed my nerves to get twisted in knots. I threw up when I got there—not too cool, but once when you become freaked out on a plane, there's not much you can do to relax.

We worked in the hospital, which was mentally tough for me. I was assigned to a pediatric oncology unit. I rocked a young boy for

155

hours because it made him feel better. I could see the challenges of being a medical professional and a parent, and I wasn't so keen on either one of them at that point in my life.

Can't Walk Out on Bob

IN 1963, SUSAN AND I WENT TO TOWN HALL to see a 22-year-old phenom named Bob Dylan. He was already iconic. I had heard him on a folk music radio station and liked him immediately.

Susan wore an orange knit suit, which made her stand out. She looked good, and I was excited to be there with her. After several songs, however, she wanted to leave, and by intermission she was insistent. I wanted to stay. Guess what happened? Bye, Bob.

When I left Susan in 1995, I wrote her a letter and placed it on the table at home, saying that I should have known that after that Dylan experience our relationship would not work in the long run.

Susan only liked classical music. She hated rock and roll. She also told me I was no basketball player, because all I did was push and shove. She was kind of right about that, but it's how I held my own with guys who were quicker, stronger, or more athletic.

It is amazing how the decision-making process works when you know nothing about the ramifications of your decision. When we married, Susan was a virtual stranger to me, as I was to her. In spite of that, the 60s became a good decade for me. Two of my children were born. Life kicked the shit out of me in more ways than one and made me more attuned to the inner me.

My Greatest Baseball Catch

I JOINED A BRITH SHALOM chapter in my neighborhood, where I met some nice men. We got together to play football every Sunday morning in the fall. I played quarterback because I had a good arm and a nice, accurate touch. It was fun. In the spring, we played in the Brith Shalom baseball league.

One Sunday, we played a double header. We lost 16 to 3 in the first game. The pitcher on the other team was excellent, and we could barely touch him for a hit. In the second game, I played center field. We were up by a run in the next to last inning. The other team loaded the bases with two outs. The pitcher from the first game was playing first base in game two. He was a very good hitter. He swung and hit a hard shot to center field. I recognized immediately it was going over my head. I ran back and soon realized I would not be able to catch the ball in my glove. I extended my right arm anyway, and the ball miraculously landed in my bare right hand instead.

The batter was decidedly upset. My teammates slapped me on the back. Even Willie Mays would have liked that catch! We held on and won the game.

Josh

SOON AFTER JOSH WAS BORN, Susan hired a woman to watch over him, which allowed her to go back to her job teaching music to students at Harding Junior High.

On one bad day, Susan made each kid write, "I must behave in class" 300 times. Her supervisor came into that class to observe, gave Susan an F and put her on probation. She finished out the year and never went back to teach again. She should have gone to teach elementary school children in the suburbs, where things were calmer. Instead, she taught private piano lessons in our home. She really needed a full-time job, and in retrospect I should have urged her more to find a teaching position in a suburban school.

Josh was a precocious child and a storehouse of information. He was very smart, if I may say so, and always seemed happy. He loved music, and we provided many children's records for him, which he memorized with ease. At age four, he could identify by name many cars we saw on the road. Today, if you ask him the nickname of any Division 1 school, chances are he will know the answer. Josh still loves music at age 53. He goes to multiple concerts a week.

When Josh was little, we bought a small, three-bedroom home at 139 Greycourt Road in the Pine Valley section of Philly. Tom Gola, one of my basketball heroes, lived less than a mile away. Tom ran a successful campaign for city treasurer one year and knocked on our front door as part of his campaign work. Susan greeted him, but I was not there. I missed my chance!

Josh was a student in the Lower Moreland school system from

kindergarten through the 12th grade. He was always a good student, but not especially great. I never checked his homework because I always had confidence he would do fine. I guess I took after my own parents in that respect, except they never really gave me much encouragement in that department. Anyway, Josh qualified for advanced placement mathematics in high school, which was no surprise given his high IQ.

One of his friends was Rod Rosenstein, who became deputy attorney general of the United States. He was our neighbor in the Albidale section of Huntingdon Valley. Josh took Nancy Rosenstein, Rod's sister, to his junior prom. Nancy later became a prominent physician.

We lived on Greycourt from 1966 to 1969. During that time, I received my CLU designation and passed the security exam to sell mutual funds. I was also offered a full-time assignment teaching social studies. The security of that position was tempting, but I decided to stop teaching and sell insurance and mutual funds.

Can't Keep Up with the Joneses

BY THE END OF 1968, Susan became pregnant with Adam, and he was born July 23, 1969. We bought a new four-bedroom home on a corner lot in Huntingdon Valley and moved in during January of 1970. It was a nice area with good schools.

What could go wrong? Everything.

The Hartford cancelled our agency because production had dipped below their new minimum. That meant four years of building an income stream was essentially gone, almost overnight. All the direct line auto insurance business was gone, too, and could not be transferred anywhere else.

Susan was no longer working, and since I had given up substitute teaching, that income was also gone. All of our neighbors were doing well. They had solid careers. I had nothing. I had never believed in selling cash value and dividends in life insurance. All my term sales were low in premiums. As a result, I was really feeling the heat.

Susan became depressed after Adam was born. I was up every four hours with his bottle and changed him, too. To me, even with my problems, he was a joy as an infant, and that joy has never abated.

Susan had suffered a miscarriage after Josh was born, and he was more than four years old when Adam was born. The two boys got along well and played together for hours once Adam became old enough. He played Little League baseball, youth soccer, and basketball. Unfortunately, due to my work schedule, I missed his best games in baseball and varsity basketball.

By that point, I had started feeling extremely anxious. Selling insurance on pure commissions and not doing it well enough was really getting to me. My mother said I didn't have what it takes to be an insurance salesman. It looked like she was right. Then my father told me something that burned into my soul right after I made him an offer.

"Hey Dad, let's work together to try and market more business," I said.

"I have enough for me," he said, "so do what you want."

That hit me hard, real hard. I think of young children whose fathers leave them. The pain must never go away. At that time, I badly needed a mentor, someone to guide me and get me on track with work. Everyone told me I would never make a living selling term life insurance. My father had sold out his casualty business. I sold mutual funds, but my prospects were drying up. My wife and I were both miserable.

What was I supposed to do now with two little children, an unemployed wife, and a new mortgage?

Susan wanted a baby girl, and I reluctantly went along with her wishes. She got pregnant again and was crushed by the news of having another boy. She wanted a daughter, not a third child.

Earlier that year, I had experienced a mental and psychological crash, and my feeling of self-worth was at ground zero. I was in bad shape and not a good candidate at all to become a father for the third time, but I thought it would make her happy.

Susan and I went to see Dr. Schall on Castor Avenue. He was Susan's gynecologist, and after taking one look at me and realizing I was in such bad shape, he offered to terminate Susan's pregnancy. She was already in her third or fourth month. We went out to the car, where Susan left it all up to me. I wasn't exactly happy to be in that position but the decision was easy to make.

"We cannot do this," I told her. "It's just plain wrong. No abortion. Period. We will have the baby."

It was the best decision of my life.

In all of our lives we make big decisions, and mine was made on a crisp, sunny afternoon on Castor Avenue.

What looked wrong surely turned out right.

Paul was born December 14, 1971. The joy he has brought cannot be fully described in simple narrative verse. He and his wife are the parents of my wonderful grandsons, Eli and Miles, who was named after Miles Davis.

Susan remained depressed and would not give Paul his bottle, so I did all the feedings. I got up every night to feed and change him. Paul was born with a small growth on his throat, which his pediatrician thought was nothing of consequence and should just be watched. The growth kept getting bigger, and by the time we finally brought him back to the doctor things had changed dramatically. The doctor realized he had made a mistake and rushed Paul to Children's Hospital of Philadelphia.

Paul stood in his crib and asked me if they were going to cut his head off. Fortunately, for all concerned, the growth was benign, but I have never trusted a doctor ever since that traumatic time.

The feeding routine went on for quite some time, and once I had a little extra money, I suggested we get out of town. Susan's parents, Adolph and Pauline, had a home in Hollywood, Florida. They lived in a community called Sheridan Lakes, with a lake for boating and a nice pool. Sometimes they invited us to visit.

During a school break during the winter term that year, we arrived one afternoon and immediately went to the pool. I was splashing around with our three boys and having fun. A little after 3 p.m., my mother-in-law came down to the pool.

"Time to get out," she said.

"Why?" I said. "We just got here, and we're all having fun."

My mother-in-law was not impressed.

"This pool is great," I told her. "This is why I paid for five round trips, which aren't cheap at the height of the season. The sun, the pool, and the fun with my kids is why we're here."

"Get out of the pool in ten minutes," she said.

Why? Why would we do this? Is this another Pearl Harbor? I didn't hear any planes overhead and saw no reason at all to stop what we were doing.

"Make sure you come inside quick and take showers," she said.

"Why now?"

"The early bird dinner at Morrison's starts at five p.m. and only lasts for half an hour, and some of the food is limited."

My wife, an only child, was a product of this family. The damage from this depression-era mentality haunted our marriage. Our children were also subjected to this behavior. With Susan, Pauline, and Adolph, life was never about pleasure. It was always about living as frugally as possible. Her parents never understood why I took the family to Florida. The food at Morrison's was awful, but we went along. After all, we were guests staying in their home.

I had been looking forward to the relief of being away from Philadelphia for a few days and all I left behind there. Earlier in 1971, I had suffered a mental breakdown and collapsed. I could not answer the phone. I had spiraled down, far away from the center of my being, and was stuck, seemingly at the bottom of an endless pit. There was only darkness in that place for me. The best part of the day was going to sleep—if I could. The depression was tangible and incredible. I went to a psychiatrist, who later committed suicide. I thought about suicide, too. I saw no way out.

We had three children, ages five and two with a baby. I had a deeply depressed wife, to boot. What was I to do? I was a guy with no marketable skills. I looked around, and the music stopped. In my mind, everyone was sitting on chairs while I was lying on the floor. If you are fortunate enough to get through this kind of darkness, something changes in you. Those people you see sleeping on benches could be you. The sadness you see in people's eyes becomes more noticeable, and you see yourself in their misery. It's as if you were there, with all that pain that immigrant families bring with them. In some weird way, it all becomes relatable.

Suicide is a terrible thing. It hurts everyone who is left behind. I understand the people who do it, however, because I faced it as a possibility. I was that low. It was on me; I created my situation. I had cut corners in school and had no ambition. No passion. Sports and music were nice, but surviving is what matters. The pursuit of happiness was no goal for me. I wasn't looking for fun. I'm still not sure I really know how to do that.

The first rule of life is learning what it takes to survive.
The second rule is, reread rule #1.

On the Job Training

I APPLIED FOR A JOB with a company named Cohen and Seltzer that were property and casualty brokers. They liked my resumé. I took a battery of academic tests and did well in all of them. Then they sent me to a psychologist, and after that I was asked to see another one. Both therapists determined (correctly) that I did not possess the self-confidence or assertiveness to be effective in the job. As a result, I was never hired.

This prompted more anxiety, which I certainly didn't need, not when things were already tight and often tense at home.

In February 1972, I received a call that saved my life. Arnie Berson was a friend of mine. He was a partner in an employment agency. Steve Duzenski was a recruiter there. He called and told me about a position at Pennsylvania Manufacturer's Insurance Company (PMA). I went to 841 Chesnut Street in the heart of Center City Philadelphia for the interview. I passed the Wunderlich test. Tom Lynch and I met, and he outlined the position. Tom was the head of a new part of the company, which is primarily a broker for workers compensation insurance and casualty insurance.

The reinsurance department was designated for property insurance and diversification. We would insure insurance companies. They would lay off some of their line in a larger portion than they originally wanted. I was a facultative underwriter. Each piece of business was offered to us, and we selected a certain amount to keep. Treaty work was different. All of the business a company wrote would become part of that.

166

I felt like a bookmaker. The offerings were from all over the country. We were offered fire-resistant office buildings and bombs that were manufactured. It was fun and definitely different. I learned on the job every day. We had guidelines for each risk category, which made the entire process very analytical. Abstract reasoning was required, and I liked that, but with the anxiety I was feeling about life in general, each day presented a struggle.

Respite from the Storm

DURING MY FORGOTTEN YEARS OF TURMOIL, I found true rest and relaxation every Friday afternoon at the Camacho baths. This was mentally helpful at a time I needed it most. They had basketball courts, a pool, and baths and showers. It was a country club for the middle class, and many guys I knew went there.

We would play half-court ball, which was exhausting *and* satisfying. No thinking was required, just playing, which provided a great respite for me from all the anxiety at work and at home.

Harold Katz, the former owner of the 76ers, played with us. This was prior to his gaining ownership, when he also had a beautiful home in Huntingdon Valley.

Harold was a decent player, but he had one basic flaw: he never passed. He only wanted to shoot. In one two-on-two game, I took the ball out every time after the opposing team made a hoop, but I never saw it back.

Basketball has virtually saved my life. I have run off large amounts of stress. I have met some great people. It is a beautiful game, especially when played as a team.

At PMA, I enjoyed the basketball games they arranged. I hadn't been there long when three senior management people challenged John Ciminera, Steve Tirney, and me to a best-of-three-games series. After giving up 15 straight points in the first game, we won two out of three. One of their guys was six foot seven and weighed 260 pounds. He went to Duke. His name was Steve Litz. I banged him around pretty good, because pushing and shoving is the key to getting rebounds and letting a guy know you won't be easy to score on. For a player like me, sometimes that's all I have going.

We played another company called Towers Perrin in football. In that game, I played quarterback and cornerback. We won on the last possession, when my friend Steve Tirney made a great catch.

The next day, my hamstrings were so stretched I could hardly walk, which lasted for a week, but it was worth it because we won!

Thank goodness for those games and the long Friday night sessions at Camacho. I would go home afterward, and for a few hours, things were manageable.

The experience made me think up a fitting aphorism:

Two essentials to man's self-confidence are a loving and devoted woman and meaningful work with adequate remuneration.

Chasing the Moon

THOSE HOURS AT CAMACHO provided a much-needed refuge, but with all the anxiety plaguing me at work, I needed my wife to provide some comfort when I was at my lowest.

"Every woman likes her husband to be financially successful," she told me.

That response to my plea was not exactly what I was looking for, but it made a clear and true statement about her priorities. Bad timing for me, but I guess she was suffering, too, in her own way.

Susan had trouble sleeping after Adam was born. She would keep me awake. Her credo was simple:

"If I don't sleep, you don't sleep."

After Paul was born in 1972, this became a serious problem. I had to be at the station to catch a 7:19 train. I slept, both going and coming home. I was a real Thomas Edison when it came to naps.

One afternoon, I fell asleep in my boss's office right in the middle of a meeting. My friend Steve Tirney woke me up. Steve later became president of PMA reinsurance after Tom Lynch left. In fact, he worked for me for a while. For a short time, I was considered the number two man. Things change. We all know that.

Working in Center City was fun. I liked that part of Philadelphia.

That year, I went to the Spectrum to see Bob Dylan (again) and The Band. Allen Flexer, the president of the Spectrum and an old basketball teammate, helped me get good seats, which were worth every penny I paid for them. What a great concert!

Years ago, during a game we played against LaSalle High School, I forgot to pack my sneakers and socks. Allen, who was a reserve, offered me his, which was an unselfish act I will always remember. As I changed on the bench, the sight of my red argyle socks gave the LaSalle fans a good laugh. I don't blame them—now. It's almost funny, too, except it's not.

Shelter from the Storm?

WHEN SUSAN WAS INITIALLY DIAGNOSED with breast cancer, it threw a big monkey wrench into our lives. Of course, every man wants a healthy wife, but life does not always provide that. I tried to be positive and supportive.

We had little to no help anywhere. At the time, we had no close friends, either. My parents offered to pay for psychiatric help, which I grudgingly admitted I needed, so I drove to Hahnemann Hospital to meet with a psychiatrist. We had four sessions. I spoke, and he stared at me; he never said a word. I drove into town once to see him for a scheduled appointment, and he wasn't in his office. He never told me he wouldn't be there. I felt abandoned. In fact, he seemed sick and demonic to me. I began to feel worse.

As Dylan said, when you get low you can always get lower. That sure happened to me during this time. Psychiatrists get paid to help you save yourself, but in my case, both of us failed to do a very good job. I really needed saving, too. Susan was handling her illness well, and I become the one feeling more out of control.

The phone call from Steve about a new job at PMA felt like he handed me a life raft. By then, I had no feeling of self-respect. I questioned if I had any marketable skills to help my family survive.

Working at PMA brought me out of that dark, self-imposed hole I had created for myself.

I started smoking on that job, though. I sat at a desk for long stretches, and it relieved the monotony. Luckily, I stopped smoking in 1976, and never smoked anything since. I was never into drugs of any kind, which was fortunate, because I didn't need any other influences tugging at my brain.

Getting myself together was a one-day-at-a-time project. The day I came home after securing my new job, Susan asked me about my salary.

"$8,800, and traditionally the company gives a 10 percent year-end bonus."

This was 1972.

"You are a Wharton graduate," she said. "That salary is an absolute insult."

One reason I had been hired was that my boss's new boss was a Wharton graduate. This kind of politics was something I did not understand at the time, like most other things outside of sports and music. I realize now that preparing for the future effectively is mandatory for maintaining long-term health and survival, but back then, I didn't really have a clue about these things.

I was not ready to be married, have children, or begin a real career.

When I began working at PMA, there were many young women employed there, and I wasn't about to complain. I was 32, and they were mostly 20 to 25. There were far more women working there than men. Some of the young woman liked me, but I was awkward, to say the least. My success with the opposite sex had not been terribly successful up until that point, especially before getting married.

To some degree, the concept of cheating was no problem for me. I was finding myself and growing as a person. My wife was giving me nothing I needed to be healthy. Before long, I was travelling in my job and ended up with a girlfriend in New York City. She wasn't too easy on the eyes, but we had fun for a while.

Years later, I met a young, attractive girl on the train to work. Her name was Dawn. She was 20 at the time; I was close to forty. She said she had lost a lot of weight, and she was quite attractive. I was flattered that she was interested in me.

173

"As 'a good German,' my father would look down on me for being friends with a Jew," she said.

I didn't let that bother me, as long as I didn't have to meet him.

The whole experience was fun and lasted about six weeks, and prompted yet another aphorism:

In life's merry-go-round,
man should spend less time groping for the brass ring
and more time examining the brass.

Games People Play

CHESS BECAME POPULAR IN THE 70s because of Bobby Fisher. One young woman in my company and I played chess at lunchtime. Under these time limitations, we often played to a draw. One day, she was docked pay because we played 10 minutes past her lunch break. I understand why the company did it, but I also think they had no appreciation for the beauty of chess.

There was special young woman at our company whom I really came to like. Her name was Joyce. She was born November sixth, making her a Scorpio, like me. I know many people scoff at the meanings ascribed to the zodiac, but I believe in the traits of each sign. I felt something special for Joyce. We played chess one day. She was winning the whole game until I beat her in the end. I could see the disappointment in her face. I asked her about baseball, and she said she found it slow and boring. We flirted all throughout the day. She wasn't especially pretty, but she was very sensual. I was attracted to her olive complexion.

She reminded me of the movie, *Room at the Top*, starring Laurence Harvey, Simone Signore, and Heather Sears. Simone was so sensual, but Laurence Harvey chose Heathers Sears because her family was prestigious and wealthy.

"What do you want, Joe?" she said to a brooding Harvey.

"I want what all the Joes want," said Harvey.

He wanted sex and money. However, he also knew that deep in his soul, he wanted to be with Simone.

I really liked that movie. For some crazy reason, I mentioned Joyce to Susan. She mocked her age and education level and my pathetic misplaced feelings. Joyce had a life outside the company. She was engaged, even though I don't remember seeing her wear a ring of any kind. I didn't wear a wedding ring because I didn't want to be typecast. I do now, but that's a story for later.

The last day I saw Joyce sticks with me, because she was about to get married and move to Columbus, Ohio. Her husband-to-be was pursuing a master's degree there. For some inexplicable reason I said something very out of character to her that day.

I've been thinking about making love to you," I said.

"I've thought about it, too," she said right back.

I kissed her goodbye. It was, and will always be, the most soulful kiss in my life. My head was virtually spinning after the experience. I called her in Columbus about a month later. She was working for the university, as I thought and hoped she might be.

"Where are you?" she said before asking me anything else.

She thought I had flown out to see her.

"I wouldn't put it past you," she said.

Goodbye Columbus was all I could say.

We never spoke again. I tried to find Joyce years later, just to see how she was doing. I called high schools in the area where she might have gone, but no luck. She suffered from seizures, so I hope she is well.

I'm glad I had the experience of finding someone to whom I felt so connected and at ease. Maybe I was just emotionally starving at that time, who knows?

Final Years at PMA

WHILE WORKING AT PMA, I visited a broker in New York who worked at Wilcox Barringer in the World Trade Center; George McCann was his name. He was a big Yankee fan. We would go to the New York Athletic Club for lunch. They had pictures of all the Heisman Trophy winners on display. They had a Pebble Beach golf course simulated on a screen. You hit the ball into the course you followed up on the screen. It was pretty neat. Fredo Genevevera was another broker I did business with, and he got us Broadway show tickets to *That Championship Season*, starring Paul Sorvino, who was very good.

I was hustling wherever I could.

In 1978, I had lunch with a neighbor named Jack Bernstein. He was an attorney working in Center City. He flipped me his life insurance policy over a tuna sandwich.

"Get me another one!" he said, instructing me to buy him another policy, as if each one cost the same as a tuna sandwich.

He purchased a $100,000 annual renewable term policy with a company called Old Line Life. Their headquarters were in Milwaukee, Wisconsin. I found an 84-year-old man in Center City who served as the general agent for that company. Through Mr. Glenn Rice, I started selling these policies to quite a few people, including some former co-workers of mine at PMA. This was before the term life insurance explosion in the early 80s. I sold enough policies to qualify Mr. Rice for a trip to Hawaii, which he was delighted about. He brought me back a small piece of coral. That was precious to me.

Glenn was tall and slim, a picture of health. He was never sick. One day, though, he didn't show up at the office. He was 86 by then. He had gone home to take a nap and never woke up. Glenn became an important bridge in my recovery. I will always remember him.

In fact, he inspired an aphorism of his own:

The success of a salesman lies not so much in his ability to read books, as in his ability to read people.

Paying for My Mistakes

I WORKED AT PMA for more than nine years, until they fired me in October 1980. I must say, they made the right decision. I had made a few serious mistakes while working there. During my second year, my boss, Tom Lynch, told us that we would be meeting Frederick Anton, the president of the company, at an upscale northern Italian restaurant. He wanted to meet all of us. The company was very Republican. I didn't know that at the time. Anton was interested to ask me about how we might grow the new reinsurance department of the company.

What did I say in ten minutes that sealed my final demise with the company seven years later?

"Uh, sir, if you don't mind my saying so, the secretaries working here are not getting a living wage, and the turnover is causing work flow problems."

He thought I was some kind of alien. After all, why would a Wharton graduate working in a Republican company give a shit about secretaries?

Every year, Frederick Anton asked my boss why Richard Krassen was still working for the company. I was naïve, but I was just being authentic. Within any team or company, the welfare of *all* the members is important to achieve success, and it must be considered. I love and respect all the virtues of capitalism, but the value and welfare of *people* must be taken into account on an equal basis. The Democratic and Republican parties have historically tried to strike a balance in this regard. When one side gets too strong, the voting public helps keep things balanced.

Fortunately, my boss defended me every year. Then, two things happened, which hurt me. I only realized that after I was excised from the company.

First, Pat McFadden, who liked me and gave me cover with my boss, left the company. Wistar Baisch, the treasurer, liked me, too, but he retired. Who was left? No one. Frederick Anton was free to vent his feelings toward me to a new boss, who realized that my time with the company was soon coming to an end.

It was partially my fault, though, that I was actually fired.

I came early to the reinsurance department. There were only three people in the whole department. My boss preached that when we became solid and successful, the salaries for all key people would rise substantially. He was right, only I was fired before that golden period began. People who worked with me and also under me for a time, reaped the rewards for a while—until they didn't.

My second mistake occurred when I shared the details of a woman's salary, someone I supervised with another female employee who sat next to me. Our conversation was made known, and my boss appropriately chewed me out for it. I had it coming.

A fellow employee and I were each assigned our own broker. My colleague liked to leave the office and take his clients golfing. He was definitely not big on pushing paperwork out in a timely manner. I went to my boss. I would do all the inside management while the other man did the traveling and the work outside the office.

That sealed my fate. I was no longer part of producing business. When another employee with an MBA was hired, I became expendable. For a while, I collected money for the department from overdue accounts. I was very good at it, which helped me keep my job for a while.

On my last day, my boss told Tony Grosso, our marketing manager, to get me Dodger tickets. Would that feed my family? That may have been the only baseball game I attended that I didn't enjoy.

I learned my lessons. Even when you work for a company, you consider yourself self-employed and plan your career successfully within the confines of the company's objectives. I never did that—or even knew I was supposed to—until it was too late, and I paid the ultimate price. BOOM! Termination. Arnold Schwarzeneggered!

My former boss once said something prophetic.

"When you feel a certain way about a person, chances are five people already figured them out in the same way ahead of you."

Smart man.

I still had a lot to learn! A few weeks after I was fired, my mother told me something very observant.

"You never would have left and gone back on your own if you hadn't been pushed out the door."

The truth was in front of my eyes. I was unconsciously behaving like my mother. I did not like anxiety or pressure. I did not like to push myself. I had no ambition, except to go through life emotionally protected.

I was almost 40, and I was a poster man for those who accepted mediocrity in all areas of life, except playing sports. I had enjoyed two decent years selling life insurance part-time before my employment fell apart. Ten years before that, I had been at the bottom. The 70s at PMA had saved my life. Over that nine-year stretch, I had started feeling better and better about myself. I made new friends, both male and female.

My last walk through the halls of the company is still clear to me. I carried a lone cigar box with my supplies. As I exited the front door, I looked up at the sky and asked God for help.

"Just give me my health, and I will take care of the rest."

My father left his job at the post office at age 40 and became modestly successful. I wanted to do better. My father did not have the passion I did. To him, the life insurance world was an income source. He was a teacher at heart. He loved teaching languages to his students. He later did that, and he finally had five happy years.

I was still looking for my happy place. I loved sports, both playing and watching. I loved music, both live and on the radio or turntable. Music has always been a major part of my life. I belonged to the opera club in high school. Mrs. Singer, our sponsor, took us to the Academy to see an opera. We sat way up top in the amphitheater, which was uncomfortable, especially considering how long an opera can be. That was a problem for me, and still is. The bigger problem, though, was finding my passion for something I was reasonably good at and that gave me the chance to make a decent living. After all, I had kids to feed!

All My Sons

ADAM SCORED HIS VERY FIRST BASKET in a community basketball game at age eight. I coached his team when he was 10, and we lost the championship game on a last second shot at the buzzer. For a hoops nut like me, that's still a painful loss.

Two years later, we finally won a championship, which I enjoyed coaching. The highlight of his community basketball career came during a best of three championship series against a team that had beaten his easily in the regular season. Adam's team lost by 15 points in the first playoff game, which, as the point guard, Adam took hard. He called me at my office and said his team had no chance to win the next game.

"They're converging on you every time down court," I told him. "Get the ball to the first open player who can shoot."

Adam did just as I suggested and by some miracle his team won the next two games. I was not the coach, but to see those other kids making shots was magical. It was the highlight of my basketball life to see them win that championship.

I liked coaching my sons' community basketball teams. Adam lost twice in the final before finally winning. I remember one loss in particular. We had a one-point lead, and a youngster named Carney made a shot at the buzzer to beat us. My assistant coach had attacked the referee on a previous play, when the ref didn't give us a call we thought we deserved, and he gave our team a double technical. The young man made both shots. My son and I still talk about it.

Losing tough ones is part of the journey.

A few years later, while I was sitting at my insurance job, Adam called. He was playing again for the championship, and it was a best of three series. In the regular league game, we lost to the same team we were competing against by 15 points. We lost the first game of the playoffs by ten.

"We're dead," Adam said. "We cannot beat that team."

"Listen, Adam, they're sending two or three players at you because they feel that only you can hurt them when it comes to scoring. So pass the ball to the closest man open at the basket."

He took my advice, and everyone began hitting their shots. We won the next two games. I was not the official coach at that time, but I was a few years later, and we won another championship.

Basketball was not the only game in town. In Lower Moreland, they had a chess club for children in our township. Mr. Hudelmeyer was a volunteer teacher. They had a ladder set up for all the kids, ranking their ability. A child could challenge a person directly above him. If he won, he would move up one position on the ladder. They met every Saturday morning during the school year. I stayed the two hours while my two youngest sons, Adam and Paul, attended.

In my humble opinion, chess is the greatest game known to man. It should be mandatory for all children to learn when they are young. The strategy concepts and the ability to analyze different ways of proceeding are valuable thinking tools.

Adam was ranked second after beating two people ahead of him. He challenged John Witty, the best in the class, and he beat him. John challenged Adam back and beat him. Adam and I still talk about a move he missed in that second game, which would have won it. I was watching that match like all the others, too.

It was a nice experience for the kids. My oldest son, Josh, is a very good chess player, too. He still plays.

My youngest son, Paul, enjoyed playing basketball, also. He can't play anymore because of back problems. Josh played very well in the community league. Once, he played great in the first half against a team we were playing for first place. The coach of the other team sent a husky boy to bang Josh around in the second half. It worked, and we lost. The boy was a drummer in the school orchestra. He was drumming on Josh, that's for sure. Scott Wister was his name.

I believe in playing to win. Always have, ever since my early days playing stickball on the streets and endless games of basketball in the local parks. However, sending in an enforcer in a community league for 11-year-olds was a little much. Mel Byck was the coach of that team, and I'd still like to give him a piece of my mind.

I took Paul for T-ball tryouts one year. It was cold and windy. Paul was given a ball and asked to throw it to the coach. He threw the ball really hard and fast, and then we ran back to the car. Paul was a first-round pick, but he never got the ball out of the infield off a tee the whole season. The following year, Paul was playing right field as I was pulling into the parking lot. Someone hit him a ball, he missed it, and I never turned off the motor. We went right out of the lot and headed home.

Very bad parenting!

Josh and Adam played on the Lower Moreland High school basketball team. They were both sixth man. Adam had one good game at Springfield. We missed it. We had tickets to the Academy of Music. I will always wish I had seen that Springfield game.

Paul had a lot of spunk and accumulated many friends. He was voted class clown at graduation. Susan, who hated to spend money, took him with her to a barber school. The students were learning, and Paul and his questionable haircuts provided a lot of laughter for his friends. They called him Bert because he had the same haircut as the Sesame Street character.

Susan taught him to play piano, which he liked. She had other students come to our home for lessons and later gave Paul jazz lessons with Curtis Harman, whose son sang with the group, Pieces of a Dream.

We had a ping pong table in our basement. We all played. No one hated to lose more than Paul, and of all three sons he had the most competitive resolve, which is still true today. He played soccer, baseball, and basketball in local community leagues. He went to chess club with Adam on Saturdays. All my sons still play chess, as does my grandson, Miles. They are all pretty good.

As a parent, I did my best to share the value of sports, including chess, with my boys, and I hope they learned all the great lessons I did from friendly competition, cut- throat gamesmanship, and the constant quest to get better at something you love.

On My Own

WHEN I FIRST LEFT PMA and tried to make it on my own, I was desperate. My judgment was a little clouded, to say the least. For example, I knew a man named Bob Phillips, whom I had met years earlier at our synagogue. He was single and taught in a local school. Every summer, at his own expense, he would take many of his inner-city students on camping trips, which they loved. We played football together every Sunday in the fall.

Out of nowhere, a lump appeared on his neck. Unfortunately, it was cancer, and he was hospitalized for treatment. He was in good spirits when I visited him in Nazareth Hospital, just east of Penney Pack Circle.

What did I bring him? A mutual fund prospectus. I was so desperate at the time, I failed to grasp that my friend was dying in front of my eyes.

The good really do die young. People you meet in life are so important, and I still needed to learn that. I had a long way to go to find my happy place.

Looking Back

A YEAR BEFORE I WAS TERMINATED, I wrote my PMA boss a detailed proposal as to why I should become an officer with the company. My boss said that what I presented was the best thing I had ever done in my eight years with the company. He said he would speak to other officers to get their feedback.

As it turned out, I was denied the opportunity I thought I deserved. After leaving the company, I engaged an old neighborhood chum to represent me in my grievance against the company. I claimed that they had discriminated against me because I was Jewish. I sat before a person from the federal government who heard my grievance. The woman was an African-American.

"How do you know for sure they were discriminating against you?" she said.

"How do you know when *you* are being discriminated against?" I said.

They settled without admitting prejudice and gave me my pension. It was ten years or nothing to get vested. There were no hard feelings. It was pure business. I saw my boss at his new job, and he gave me two life insurance leads, which led to new sales.

Maybe I was lucky to get fired when I did, so I could leave that place for greener pastures. The truth is, I was never a corporate guy. At times, I would not dress conservatively, as expected. I challenged management decisions. My boss said I had a great sense of urgency. He would show me complicated proposals from brokers of ceding companies. I almost never liked them. The risks for the reward was not attractive to me. Sometimes he listened to me and sometimes he did not.

There were a few ironies after I was fired. The man who took my place, Bill Fullerton, wrote a letter to top management about all the bad things my boss had done. My boss was removed shortly after, and Fullerton left the company, too.

In the nine years I worked at the company, we always made money. The reinsurance department went out of business after I left. Within a year, the three people who worked in that department and had been there before me all left. I don't know why. In any case, I learned a lot from things going south.

Failure is a great teacher and mind changer.

Let's say you have an injury that never heals. No matter how much healing you do in the future, demons from the past remain in your consciousness. To this day, I don't sleep well, and I am very anxious a great deal of the time. There is no logic on the surface, but as you peel away the layers, the truth becomes obvious.

We all have pain we try to manage and bury.

Many thriving businesses feed off the afflictions of those with mental problems. The pharmaceutical industry offers a plethora of drugs to reduce depression and anxiety. The alcohol industry wants to help make you feel good and numb the pain. Vacation travel tries to seduce you to make you happy and give you a chance to escape—– or at least try to—from your fears and uncertainty.

The only answer to me is embracing the pain, fear, and uncertainty that have stalked me for so many years. I write about it, try to understand it, and attempt to do things each day that are honest and make me feel better about myself.

Many years ago, I wrote a short little story, trying to describe the struggle I was having with my own identity:

The Chase

I hated him at first, knowing he was following me, haunting me, stalking me, driving me to moments of insanity. For more years than I care to admit, I hated him, repressed feelings about him, and hid whenever he was coming.

At times, he would call to me strange things like, "Don't be afraid of the truth, don't be afraid." This strange, absurd, incongruous creature of the night would call out, "I'm your best friend." I knew differently. The bastard was trying to kill me, destroy me, rob me of what little I had.

There were times I would travel — London, Bermuda, Puerto Rico — and still he was there. Instinctively, he would know where I was. The crazy thing was, the harder I tried to forget him and the harder I ran, the worse he tormented me. It was as if he was trying to inflict some cruel punishment on me.

"Why me, why me?" I cried out, but he wouldn't go away.

"Please," I begged, "leave me alone, let me be. I'm satisfied with my life."

The son of a bitch wouldn't stop.

"You are a Scorpio, don't be afraid. You must be brave. I am your best friend."

Then, finally, it happened some four years ago: I was down, I couldn't move, and he started to come closer.

"Get the fuck away from me, you ugly charlatan," I cried.

All of a sudden, gradually really, I came to see that he would not hurt me if I didn't let him. For some strange reason, whenever I was very honest about my thoughts and feelings, we felt very close.

Then one day, he implored me to touch his face, to listen to his voice. And although still scared, I did it. This seemingly complex apparition was really quite human and gentle. After we became friends, he gave me a mirror.

190

"Look in it," he said, "and you will see both of us."

This was a strange request, but reluctantly, I complied. With a chill, with a cringing terror, I looked. And to both my delight and horror, it was I, standing all alone.

The painful yet joyous realization captured in that short story encapsulates much of what I was going through in my life during those up and down years. I learned so much when I finally started paying close attention. We cannot let other people define us. We have to challenge ourselves from a young age to identify our strengths and build on them. We must acknowledge the things we are no good at and get other people or technology to help.

Good advice and mentoring are among the most precious things on earth after meeting our survival needs. And the quest to get better never ends!

Reality

Seeing the sun without a glare,
A goddess with silk black hair,
Romping in the sun without a care,
Her skin so soft, so fair …

A clanging on my right,
Suddenly has me uptight,
My eyes open wide,
It's panic inside …

The important decree:
Don't miss the seven thirty-three.

Maybe tonight after my head hits the pillow,
I'll conjure a glimpse of a huge weeping willow.

Grabbing a rebound during a faculty-student game
in 1966 at George Washington High School,
where I worked as a substitute teacher.
We won!

Adam's Bar Mitzvah, 1981.

1117 Ashbourne Road, Huntington Valley,
home with Susan, Josh, Adam and Paul, 1970 to 1995

Temple Shalom, where Susan and I were married in 1964,
and where I had my Bar Mitzvah in 1953.

Susan and I on our wedding day, 1964.

PART THREE
Coming of Age

A Love Affair Meets New Challenges

ON SEPTEMBER 16, 1980, I was fired from my position as manager of the reinsurance department at PMA Insurance Company. I was evicted from the office I had occupied for nearly nine years. Fully aware that this would be the last time, I walked to the train station to return home with a cigar box under my arm, full of the personal belongings I had kept with me at work all of those years. They had been kept in a desk that now was no longer mine.

As I walked, clutching almost a decade of memories along with that box, I knew that I had to find a new work home, somewhere I could thrive without all the palace intrigue. This was not as intimidating as I might have thought, because I realized that I was older and wiser now, and I had more self-confidence than I had previously enjoyed. It was clear that there were life insurance products in the marketplace to be excited about, ones that were not available in the 60s, but which I could capitalize on now. I had been selling life insurance part-time from 1997 to when I lost my full-time job at PMA.

I was ready to embark on a new life, or so I thought.

1980 was definitely a good year for professional sports teams in Philadelphia. They were all doing well at the same time, which was highly unusual. The Eagles, 76ers, and Phillies all played for the championship that year. The Phillies won their first World Series just weeks after I was fired. The city was floating with good cheer.

I had reason to feel good, even though I had no job and was still recovering from a surgical procedure I'd had the year before. I woke up early one morning and became scared when I discovered blood coming from my rectum. I had no idea how something like that could be happening. I went to Abington Hospital later that day, when my fear of the unknown became unbearable. I was told I had a bad case of hemorrhoids, which needed immediate attention. A doctor rubber-banded them, which was very unpleasant and something I am loath to explain in any detail.

I was not alone in my situation. In 1980, during one of his great Hall of Fame seasons, George Brett, the star for the Kansas City Royals, made hemorrhoids famous when he announced he had them and was taking care of them like a champ. I felt like if he could deal with them, so could I. Who cares if I have no income and a sore butt? I was determined to turn around my firing and physical folly and get my life together.

My optimism was tempered soon enough by the realities I faced at home. I could not avoid the numerous negative forces that seemed to be surrounding me on all sides. No matter how I tried to spin it, nothing could change the fact that I now had three sons, ages 15, 11, and nine. My wife did not work outside the home and brought in no income. It was up to me to start working at a level of intensity that I had avoided until that time. I wasn't sure what I would do, but I knew I had to throw myself into the challenge by dedicating every waking hour of every day to making a success of my second go-round in the business. I was hoping that if I pushed hard enough, I might improve my chances for good luck.

As a result, the 1980s became a coming of age for me.

Learning My Lessons

CONTROL YOUR ENVIRONMENT. I learned that from my mother, not my father. She always had a handle on how to take charge of her immediate surroundings. Those daily naps she took when I was a young child, when she closed the door and left me to my own devices, were an example of controlling her environment. It was now my turn to learn those lessons myself.

Do not do anything that will cause fear, uncertainty, and pain. That was a golden rule for people less golden than me. I was not different from anyone else, as I had no desire to attract fear, uncertainty, or pain, but the business I was in relied on all three of those factors. Selling life insurance is all about channeling the emotions of fear, uncertainty, and pain. You work on pure commission. You only get paid when a policy is signed, sealed, and paid for on delivery.

Protect yourself at all times. That's the key—playing the risk factor. Most people can't handle too much risk. That's why the insurance business is so large and penetrates most every aspect of our lives. For me, it certainly did, and I had my share of ups and downs, as reflected in a poem I wrote in 1975 (next page), looking at the high times I enjoyed while knowing they do not last as long I'd like.

RICHARD G. KASSEN

Yuppie's Lament

Age 35, an Ivy degree,
Make lots of money, the important decree.

A home in the suburbs, a large swimming pool,
Our only child in a private school.

American Express Gold, a BMW in the drive,
These are the necessities that keep us alive.
It happened over three months ago,
They called us in, as business was slow,

Unfortunately, some of us had to be let go,
It's not easy finding work, you know.
It looks like our life will need some rearranging,
As in Dylan's lyrics, "The times, they are a-changing."

When It Gets Personal

MY MOTHER LIVED UNTIL AGE 96. She never worked outside the home. While she had lessons to teach, she was actually a bad role model for me once I had a family to support. She always wanted me to play it safe, so as not to cause *her* any anxiety.

Now that I was on my own, I needed to buckle down and find my own way in my chosen field. There are business advantages to selling life insurance that are different from other businesses. There are no tracks to run on. For example, in medicine, law, or accounting, there are prescribed ways to get a formal, approved education, prepare through internships of all kinds, and work toward your goal through a conventional career ladder.

Selling insurance is a different animal. There is little overhead needed. One needs no employees or costly equipment and inventory. You just have to find people to talk to and convince that you have something they need. Most people have a need for life insurance. They may not know it at first, so it's my job to help them understand it. The money is paid in lump sums, tax free, free of probate fees, and free of creditors.

People who sell it must be self-starters and have tremendous emotional endurance. People do not like to be reminded that they will die. They do not like spending money for a benefit that is not meant to be directly for them. They look at the monthly or quarterly premiums as an expense, and in some cases, a burden.

I read the obituaries every day. At least three or four times a week someone young passes away and leaves a family behind. In most cases, they ask that memorial contributions be paid to their children's education fund. They had little or no life insurance. They loved their kids but lived with one outstanding flaw. They never could acknowledge that they could die prematurely without a ton of money in the bank or any other sizeable assets.

The other unfortunate piece of the equation is that they never bought a policy from a life insurance agent or broker. This is a product that is sold. Many people only have coverage because some persistent agent sold it to them.

Instead, most people flood to Starbucks, where they spend money every day on overpriced, fancy coffee instead of what they should be providing for their family. Some of those people complain that they have no money for life insurance. Then some of them die before their time and ask others to help subsidize their children's higher education.

I sell term insurance, or lifetime coverage without savings in the contract. There are many fine companies that sell whole life and do a very fine job for themselves, their agents, and their policyholders. I sell the tax-free death benefit. The dollars put into the contract are a small percentage of the face value of the policy. People should be insured for at least ten times their annual income. Life insurance is designed to replace income that would have been otherwise earned if the decedent had lived.

Sol Hebner at the University of Pennsylvania called it the *human life value concept*. I still sell the products as I learned about them from the original master of this academic approach. He cited the many wealthy people who buy large amounts of coverage. They have plenty of money and assets to burn. Why do they do this? They know the payoff is tax-free and the cost to life expectancy is very aggressively priced.

Few people would want or be able to sell life insurance. The knowledge necessary to sell the product is within reach of almost everyone, yet not everyone sees it in himself or herself to sell it.

That's because the tough part of the whole occupation is the pain of being rejected almost all the time. People will ignore you or show complete apathy when they are approached. People whom you sell to are also reluctant to refer you to a business colleague, friend, or family member. That is a real problem, as word of mouth is so vital in most every business.

Without leads, a life insurance salesman is dead in the water. This is when it becomes a very lonely business. We say it's a pure survival business.

If you sell, you eat, and your family eats, too.

If you don't sell, you don't eat, and your family is hungry and upset.

Susan was not exactly supportive whenever I would voice any type of frustration.

"You picked it," she said. "So face it; there are no other choices for you."

She was being honest, but I was upset. I had to apply all of the aggressive behavior, persistence, and passion I had learned playing basketball and apply it to selling insurance.

"You hated getting in arguments when you were young," my mother told me. "You turned away from verbal confrontations."

I had no clever comeback. Verbal confrontations had become part of my life, but I was optimistic that this time I would be successful. In order to be effective at selling life insurance, certain factors must be in place. Most important is believing that what you do has value. I can get rejected fifty straight times, and I will still go after the fifty-first opportunity because I believe in myself, my products, and the value of what they will do for the buyer. However, the uncertainty of where your next sale will come from is a constant problem. When selling term insurance, most companies pay out the entire commission in the first year. You then service 19 years of a 20-year contract with no further compensation.

People selling whole life insurance receive nine years of renewals. This allows the agent to build a renewal base of income. In all businesses, the reliance on repeat business is mandatory to survival. Doctors, dentists, and CPAs all have patients and clients who see them on a prescribed basis. Restaurants need repeat customers. Drug companies pursue continuing use of their drugs. This type of rolling customer base makes these businesses thrive.

The lack of the ability to resell is a big problem for me. The successful salesman needs creative ways of developing a client base. I am not complaining. Every occupation and job has its own distinct problems. Working for someone else presents its own set of problems, too. The company, or your particular boss, sets the culture. When I worked for PMA, I had to become part of the company culture to be ultimately successful. When I couldn't do that in a way that was satisfactory for them, I was terminated.

While selling insurance may feel like something quite anonymous to most people, I have always considered it to be quite personal. I received my original license to sell life insurance in 1963. Fifty-five years later, I'm still here, selling life insurance. You could say I could write a book about it!

I've sold for numerous companies and they have paid out many claims. Only once in 55 years has a beneficiary called and thanked me for selling their loved one a policy. Of course, I received a commission for making the deal, but don't you thank your doctor after he or she helps you? Don't you send an acknowledgment to your CPA when they get you through a complicated tax return? What about your housecleaner or trainer or delivery boy?

Does it hurt? Yes, it does.

What's It Worth?

INSURANCE IS DEEPLY PSYCHOLOGICAL. Because of that, there is one essential point every life insurance salesman must remember. All the apathy, avoidance, and rejection they experience is *not* about the salesman. It is the total psychological approach to the process.

Most people who are approached to purchase life insurance are not in the market to buy it. This is not something most people wake up to on any given day and put on their To Do list.

Mow the lawn.

Get your wife flowers.

Purchase life insurance.

I don't think so.

Any life insurance salesman can sell to a person who is already in the market to buy. In those cases, it can be a slam-dunk process and almost too easy to enjoy. On the other hand, people become disturbed, angry, and downright pissed off when someone like me tries to approach them. They don't return calls and avoid responding to emails. In the old days, people answered their phones. Now they don't. It is much harder now. A salesman lives for leads and opportunities to sell, but these opportunities are getting tougher by the day to come by.

Who needs a real person? I've got an insurance app.

In one of Woody Allen's movies, a man is locked in a cell with a life insurance salesman as punishment. It's very funny. I take this stuff quite seriously, but when Woody goes after it with his eagle eye, even I have to laugh. It can be a psychological nightmare—for both parties!

When you sell, you make your points as succinctly as possible. You listen to the prospect. You find their comfort spot and make the sale. Sometimes, in fact pretty often, you have to disturb the prospect. He or she may simply need to get into what I affectionately call *the discomfort zone*.

Being liked is not the goal.

Showing a prospect the need and finding the right price is essential. Many times, a prospect will refuse to acknowledge the need or value of the product. In that case, when you've given it your best effort, you move on.

The best prospects are those who have bought life insurance in the past. The hardest ones are those people who have never bought life insurance or even considered it.

I had an office in my basement in Huntingdon Valley, with a little window high in the corner. It was similar to the cell Burt Lancaster occupied in the movie *Bird Man*. I had no birds to take care of, but I had five hungry mouths to feed.

For me, finding success at selling life insurance was a matter of life or death.

Life Goes On

DURING THE 70S AND 80S and well into the 90s, we were members of The Dolphin Swim Club, located just outside the city in Lower Bucks County. Members were assessed a bond payment upon joining, which was held by the club and returned when the membership was ended.

There was a yearly fee per family, but it was something I could afford, and the whole place was very attractive to our family. It gave us a nice place to go in the summertime when the pool and tennis courts were both open and full of activity. There was a snack bar, and basketball courts, too, which I was especially happy to see.

Some men at the club bought life insurance from me. Meeting people under the right circumstances is vital to the success of my business. I once met a man at Dolphin named Paul Denish. He and his wife, Carole, became clients and friends of mine.

Our three sons found plenty to keep themselves occupied. I played volleyball with friends every Saturday and Sunday. Volleyball is a great game. I enjoyed the dink shot the best. When standing up at the net, instead of spiking the ball, I would just hit it, so it just barely went over the defender and dropped behind him.

One time, a man on the other team hit the ball with such force that it split my fingers and caused a huge gash. Blood was spouting all over the court. My wife drove me to the emergency room; after waiting a considerable amount of time, they finally sewed me up. I couldn't play again for two weeks.

I often got into three-on-three basketball games, forming a team with Josh, my 13-year-old, and Adam, my nine-year old, to play against three grown men. We usually won. Once, a man named Mel called an illegal pick on Adam. He challenged a nine-year-old about the winning basket. I screamed at him and we went back and made another basket and won the game.

After the game, Josh said I embarrassed him with my yelling, and I'm sure he was right, but we won the game!

They had a tennis tournament for the boys. Adam made it into the final for a best of five set match. He played a boy who was on his high school team. Adam won the first two but lost the last three. Unfortunately, he lost the momentum he had built up in those first two sets and played those last three trying not to lose instead of finishing off the win. The whole club was watching. I think the moment was too much for him. I was very proud of him, though, and hope he still knows that today.

My children played community basketball in the gym of The Red Lion School in Lower Moreland. The men there started a four-on-four league, playing full court on the side baskets. We didn't run the regulation full court. We had really good players, and it was a great deal of fun. I played pickup ball there on Saturday afternoons. League games were every Tuesday night. We won the championship game in 1980 by 28 points and all got championship jackets. As a kid I had always wanted one of those, and I enjoyed it just as much as an adult.

Arnie Aronovitz, a great player and teammate on our championship team, suggested that I should get into the over-30 league at the Klein Branch of the Jewish Y. I joined in 1981 and stayed for 31 years until the age of 72.

My friend Norty Levine was a basketball legend in Philadelphia. He recently turned 84 years old and still plays forward in an over-55 league with his son, Mitchell, who is the high scorer in the league. Norty has almost no body fat and can rebound and play great defense. He has a good mid-range shot and a nasty hook. In many games throughout the years, Norty and I played head to head and enjoyed memorable battles. Norty also played with Dan Fleming in numerous three-man tournaments, and one year they were national champs!

When the Jewish Basketball League gave me my award, Norty introduced me and talked about how tough I was and how my nickname was Krassen the Assassin. His respect has always meant a great deal to me. I have never met anyone who loves playing basketball more than Norty.

Basketball has kept me sane throughout my life.

Feeding the Family

I HAVE A LONG-TIME FRIEND FROM HIGH SCHOOL whose name is Ed Biasi. He is a Drexel University graduate who went to work for Sunoco at Three Penn Center in Center City. I spoke to him about life insurance. He had a group life insurance policy with his company. I told him since he was a healthy non-smoker, I could save him money. We agreed that we would speak the following Tuesday. On Monday afternoon I called him. He said he had decided to keep the group deal for himself and that he had handed in the paperwork that same morning.

"Eddie, go back and get that form," I said, "and let me save you money."

Thank goodness he agreed, and I wrote up an application. He then told three key executives at Sunoco that he was working with me because of my ability to save him money. News got around the company, and I became the man to see.

I went to Marcus Hook and sold to many employees there. I had a man named Jeffrey Parkins, who would wake up early and do exams in their offices to determine policy details. He is presently a successful real estate broker in Jenkintown, Pennsylvania. I could not have done this effectively without him. I eventually wrote more than 80 contracts from Sunoco employees.

Nests like these, where you can get multiple clients in one location, are essential when it comes to selling life insurance. I developed other nests with employees who worked for the city of Philadelphia, the Environmental Protection Agency, and a drug enforcement unit of the federal government. Many employees from PMA, my old company, also became clients. My deceased friend, Alan Gart, helped me gain access to talk to people in the actuarial department at Cigna Insurance Company.

As a freelance salesman, I worked seven days a week. I wasn't only doing it for my family. I was doing it for me.

One hot day in August, my mother told me it is so hard to sell life insurance in very hot summer weather. I told her there are good reasons all year long why it's a bad time to sell life insurance."

"Believe me," I said. "There's no way I'm looking for any new reasons to fail."

At the time, A.L. Williams was a company in the news. They had part-timers telling everyone to buy term insurance and invest their money with the difference they saved. People were cashing in old whole life insurance policies. They were waking up to buying large amounts of term coverage at very low premiums. I was in at the right place at the right time.

There are many fine agents who sell for great companies that sell whole life insurance. They believe in building savings in your policy. I do not believe in that concept, but I respect people who do. Life insurance should be purchased for the lump sum, tax-free benefit, which pays off at the time of death. The cost never approaches the face. I could go on and on, but the details of the business are not the most important point. What means the most to me, looking back over all these years in the business, is that selling life insurance has been very good to my family and me.

I am essentially a broker who shops for a client to find the best rates with the best companies. That's what all the nuances of this work boils down to: good value for a good investment.

My bread and butter company continues to be Cincinnati Life. I have been writing policies for them for 18 years and they are a wonderful company.

I would like to feel I have been a credit to the business. There has been frustration and failure and joy, but I know I am doing a service. Through my efforts of over 55 years, there are people left behind with the necessary funds to survive. The companies represented by me have paid out millions of dollars in death benefits. My loved ones and I have enjoyed many benefits from my pursuing this profession.

Cashing In

THE TIMES WERE RIGHT, and I was finally ready. During the 80s, many companies awarded trips to their most productive producers. In my second year back working full-time, I qualified for a trip to Casa del Sol in Spain. I was placing my business through a Shelly Blanks company called Brokers Insurance Services. I became a general agent for Great Southern Life and Midland National and qualified for a trip to Hong Kong, China, and Japan. I was also winning rings and watches for my production.

All through these years, I pushed myself and was fortunate to get excellent results. Luckily, I followed my own nose and carved out quite a business for myself.

Back in 1964, shortly after getting my license, I had a seven o'clock appointment one evening on Algon Avenue. It was a very cold February night. There was ice on the ground and barely anyone on the road. I arrived on time, knocked on the door, and no one answered. I waited a while before heading back to my car to go home. I knew the prospect was home. No one was out and about on night like that, not even in Philadelphia, where people are used to bad weather in the winter. I called when I got home. The man said he was in the shower and had not heard me.

Why hadn't his wife answered the door? Were they taking a shower together at seven in the evening? I didn't forget his name. In fact, I went back and sold him a policy.

Jim Martin, a high school friend of mine, referred me to his brother. I sold him a $50,000 term policy, which was a nice amount back in the 60s. Sadly, he had a bleeding ulcer and died one year after the policy went into effect. I went to the funeral with no idea that his wife would disappear shortly after collecting the money.

Years later, I was watching another frustrating Phillies game on television when I got a call that a client named Steve Berg had died. He was a young man, no more than 35 years old. I wanted to do the right thing, so I drove to Southampton, where the family was sitting Shiva.

Steve's father-in-law mocked me because he thought Steve should have had more coverage. That type of cold attitude, especially after such a young man had tragically died, was very unpleasant for me.

"Your son-in-law was an engineer," I said. "He told me the exact amount of coverage he wanted, and I arranged it for him."

I left immediately afterwards, shaken to my core and wondering how people learn to behave the way they do. I guess stress can make people lose their character and sense of values.

I always remember the sales that got away as much as the ones I made. Anyone in the business remembers. It happens to all of us. Fortunately, most did not get away, and my memories of those times are largely quite good.

What Really Matters

IN 1980, THE PHILLIES FINALLY WON a World Series. I had just lost my job, so I was too preoccupied to fully enjoy it. The city was jubilant. Everyone seemed all keyed up to go to the parade. I never went. I was too busy figuring out how to feed my family. I wasn't exactly in the mood to process what this victory represented for those of us who had grown up watching so many losing teams.

I remember all the bad, painful losses prior to the joys of 1980. One in particular had occurred in 1958, during the first game of a Sunday doubleheader in County Stadium against the Milwaukee Braves. They had a terrific team, which won the championship the previous year but lost it in '58 to the New York Yankees.

I was in Moorestown, New Jersey at the time, visiting Sylvia Denbo, a friend of my mother's since their childhood in Scranton. Sylvia's husband, Sydney, was a successful dentist, and they had a beautiful property with a big apple orchard. My cousin, Jerry Meyer, and I started throwing apples at Sylvia's sons, Jay and Michael. We were enjoying the sport of taunting them, when out of nowhere another boy from the neighborhood joined them. He started throwing apples really with both hands! I had never seen anything like this before. We ran for cover and learned a life lesson that day before settling in to enjoy the game.

The starting pitcher for the Phillies was Herman Wehmeier. Herm had been viewed as a boy phenom in Cincinnati, and I believe the Reds signed him at age 15 or 16. He never fulfilled his promise, so they traded him to the Phillies. He was magnificent that day. The Braves managed just a few hits, and hardly any of them were hit hard.

The Phillies built up a 3-0 lead heading into the bottom of the ninth. There was no reason to bring in a relief pitcher. No one worried about a pitch count back then. The Braves loaded the bases on a walk and some lucky hits that found holes. Then Herm got two outs before Del Crandall, the Braves catcher, came up to bat. He got behind in the count, but then Herm made a lethal mistake. He threw an inside fastball, and Crandall crushed it for a grand slam homerun. It was shocking. I'm sure Herm never forgot it. Robin Roberts, the great Phillies pitcher, remembered all of his tough losses but this was different. Herm was pitching a masterpiece. Not a Harvey Haddix masterpiece, but a brilliant performance, nonetheless.

I have seen the Phillies lose many times on walk-off hits, but I have never seen them lose like they did that day.

In 1961, the Phils had a dreadful team and lost 23 games in a row. I was listening to the game on the radio when they finally broke that streak in the second game of a Sunday doubleheader against the Braves, when they won 9-3. Johnny Buzhardt was our starting and winning pitcher.

Following the Phillies—for better or worse— seemed to be a birthright for anyone who was born in Philadelphia. When I was 10 years old, our family normally met at my grandparents' home in the Logan section of Philadelphia on Sundays.

On one beautiful, sunny Sunday in August, the Phillies were playing the New York Giants. Everyone was going to the Philadelphia Zoo. I loved the zoo, but I wanted to stay and watch the doubleheader. Everyone urged me to come to the zoo. I was resolute and held to my guns. The Phillies were more important, so I stayed and followed the games. They got shut out in two gut-wrenching defeats. Everyone had a great time at the zoo, except for me, but suffering along with my team came first, and this devotion made me a die-hard fan for life.

Did He Really Catch It?

BASEBALL IS A SLOW, ANALYTICAL SPORT. It is like chess. Each move is significant. Hitting a baseball is hard, especially at the major league level. The game has changed significantly. The money is way bigger. The cost to go to the game is considerably more. Back in the day, I took my three sons to games, and you could get a good seat for $15. The cost for a family today is beyond the budget of many fans. That's sad, and I don't think it's particularly good for the game.

The players are different now, too. In the old days, baseball meant everything to the players, but they needed part-time jobs in the off-season. There were fewer teams and fewer players reached the majors. Many AAA minor league teams had terrific players.

The leadoff men would do anything to get on base. The number two hitters could hit behind the runner. Number three was usually your best hitter. The cleanup man knocked in runs.

The Phillies had a player named Granny Hamner who played shortstop. He hit about .260 or .270. He was a great clutch hitter, though, and when we needed a big hit, he would often deliver. He sticks out for me because of the way he could hit under pressure.

One loss will always stick with me. It was on Memorial Day in 1954. We were playing the Brooklyn Dodgers at home. The lead changed many times, and the game continued to be more and more exciting. I was outside playing and missed some of it.

A Dodger named George "Shotgun" Shuba got a big hit and put the Dodgers up going into the bottom of the ninth. Our first two batters were retired. The next two walked. In came Clem Labine, the

Dodgers best relief pitcher. Willie "Puddin' Head" Jones was our next hitter. The count went full, and Labine grooved one. Jones really connected. I thought it was going to be a home run, but the ball did not quite have home run distance. It was heading like a missile for the top of the wall. If it hit there, both runners would have scored, because with two outs they were running on the pitch.

Then Duke Snyder, the Dodger centerfielder, took off on a dead run and caught the ball up against the wall. I thought he might have trapped it, but Jones was called out. Many years later, Duke was asked if he caught that ball, and he never answered. I guess we will never know.

Football Rules in Philly!

PHILADELPHIA IS A FOOTBALL TOWN. Football rules. There are Phillies fans and Flyers fans and 76er fans, but Eagles fans rule the roost, especially now, after winning the Super Bowl. On game day, people arrive several hours before kickoff. They drink, tailgate, eat, and listen to music. They all wear Eagles gear. Some paint their faces green. If you show up at an Eagles game in a jersey from another team, you do so at your own peril. It is like going to the zoo and getting too close to the gorillas. I don't recommend it. In fact, it shouldn't be that way. We should all respect people from out of town who come to Philly to watch their team. But that's not the case, especially with teams in our division. For example, if you wear a Cowboys jersey on a Sunday in Philly, you must have a death wish. Eagles fans hate the Cowboys even worse than the New York Giants. I think I know where it started, but I'm not sure.

Back in the day, we had a fan favorite named Timmy Brown. He was a great looking guy and a terrific football player. On one play, on a crossing route coming out of the backfield, his jaw met the forearm of a Dallas linebacker named Lee Roy Jordan. Brown was laid out cold. Ever since, we all hate Dallas. Troy Aikman, the Dallas quarterback, used to take a beating from our players. Buddy Ryan, our former coach, used to promise that we wouldn't lose to Dallas, and I don't think we ever did when he was our coach.

In 1980, we beat Dallas in the conference final and were the favorites when we played the Oakland Raiders in the Super Bowl.

They dominated the Eagles, and we lost. It was never close, which made it even tougher to take. We had beaten this team at home in the regular season, but on that day in New Orleans, in a low-scoring game, the Raiders were the better defensive team and never let us get going like we had proven we could. The Eagles had a very fine offensive line, but Jaworski, our quarterback, was rushed that day on every play and could never execute at his normal level.

Following the season, some of the members of the Eagles came to Lower Moreland High School to play a basketball game against some community players to raise money for charity. Each participant for Lower Moreland had to pay to participate in the game. The cost was too much for me, but at the last minute, one of my neighbors, Steve Clyman, had to skip the game because of a bad back. Steve and I had played high school basketball together at Lincoln. He asked me if I would take his place, which I was happy to do. The players from the Eagles were very big, and some of them were good basketball players.

I played my usual hustling style, rebounding and playing hard. The next thing I knew, a three- hundred-plus-pound lineman came up behind me at mid court. He wrapped his huge arms around me, and I couldn't move, although I certainly tried. There was great laughter in the stands. It was all a fun experience. We later played a game against Lower Moreland faculty, which was also a lot of fun.

I loved watching pro football. I also loved playing touch. I had a good arm and could catch anything thrown near me while I played end. I never went out for the high school team. I was conscious of the risk of getting hurt. I never played tackle football, either. Lincoln High School had great football teams when I attended there. In my sophomore year, we lost a close game to North Catholic for the city championship. In my junior year, the team beat LaSalle 28-20 to capture the city championship.

There were some great games, too, against our biggest rival, Frankford High School. I will never forget one remarkable game. They were up 7-0 at halftime. Our head coach was a man named

Moe Weinstein. We had a terrific athlete playing quarterback, whose name was Bill "Pickles" Kennedy. In the second half, we went from a T-formation to a single-wing formation, and every snap went directly to Kennedy. He scored three touchdowns, and we won 19 to 7. Frankford knew where the play was going on every play, but they still could not stop us.

Kennedy was arguably the finest athlete ever to attend Lincoln High School. Larry Cannon was a close second. Kennedy was also the starting point guard on Lincoln's basketball team. He went to Temple and teamed up with Guy Rodgers to create a great backcourt combination. He also played in the Pittsburgh Pirates' minor league system. Kennedy died in Florida some years back and left us all some great memories.

When I went to Lincoln and played JV basketball, my first cousin, Miles, saw Bill "Pickles" Kennedy on a bus. He knew I played at Lincoln. He told Pickles he was my first cousin.

"Richie Krassen is your cousin?" said Pickles.

Miles got really excited and said yes.

"He sucks!" Pickles said.

Miles told me this, word for word, and it still makes me laugh. It is somewhat ironic that I played a game against Pickles in the summer of 1959. He brought an all-star team to Camp Green Lane to play our team. My former teammate, Bruce Drysdale, who later starred at Temple, was on his team. Ernie Beck, the great All-American from Penn, was playing for Camp Green Lane. I started and played the whole game. We lost by ten. Ernie had 20 points. I had 15 points. Luckily, I made sure I didn't suck that night.

Bring on the Hoops!

THE 1980S WAS A SIGNIFICANT DECADE in my continuing love affair with the game of basketball. I watched, played, and coached. I loved watching high school, college and professional games.

The 76ers were regularly in contention for a championship during those years. In 1980, they lost to Los Angeles in six games. The legendary Magic Johnson scored 42 points playing center in the deciding game six. Kareem Abdul Jabbar had a severe migraine and did not play, but Magic rose to the occasion and did his thing, earning himself a guaranteed spot in the Hall of Fame.

In 1981, we had a great chance to go to the championship round, but the Boston Celtics beat us in the Eastern division finals. In 1983, we finally broke through and won the championship when we swept the Lakers in four straight. We had a terrific team that year, led by the one and only Dr. J.—Julius Erving, who could take over a game all by himself.

The Celtic-Laker rivalry was great to watch. Later, it became the bad boy Pistons that won two championships. I loved watching that team play such a physical style. Bill Lambier set great picks. He could shoot from the outside. He was an excellent rebounder. Players on other teams hated him. I liked that.

When I wasn't busy trying to sell life insurance, I spent much of my leisure time watching basketball. College basketball was something I cared about and watched, too. The upset of

Georgetown by Villanova in 1985 will always be a lasting memory. Villanova was a #7 seed and was given a very slim chance to win. They beat a great Georgetown team, which should have pressed the whole game. By upping the tempo, they would have won. They had better athletes and a better bench. They let Villanova, which shot over 70 percent, set the tempo.

However, the greatest college basketball story was not Villanova. North Carolina State had a coach named Jim Valvano. He coached in what was probably the toughest conference at that time. Virginia had Ralph Sampson. Michael Jordan was at North Carolina. Duke was always tough. North Carolina State did not qualify for the tournament, based on their play in the regular season. They had to win their conference championship playoff to even get in. They played three really good teams and beat them all in close games.

Jim Valvano did something so amazing. He had his team cut down the nets on the rims *before* the season even started. He wanted his team to feel what it would be like to win a national championship and celebrate with that tradition. His coaching was outstanding. He directed each play from the sidelines. He had his players foul players on the other teams who had a high likelihood of missing their free throws. They did miss at key times, too.

They made it to the national tournament, won every game and got to the final where they played Houston. Three players from Houston later played in the NBA. Watching that game was a real delight. There was a controversial charging call against Clyde Drexler. That play gave him four fouls. Lorenzo Charles put in the winning basket off an air ball just before the buzzer.

In 1981, I joined the Klein Branch of the JCC, which was located close to the intersection of Red Lion Road and Bustleton Avenue. In the mid-70s, they started an over-30 basketball league with two courts that were not quite regulation size, which meant we didn't have to run as much and could play two twenty-minute halves without collapsing. We had twelve teams competing in two divisions for a championship.

The great thing about this league was the common draft they instituted to get it all started. The players were seeded one through eight, depending on their abilities. Each of the twelve teams had a captain who selected his team. The goal was to make each round fair, with a balance of talent. After each round, an impartial league official adjusted each pick for each captain, based on the perceived strength of each team.

Everyone knew the strengths and weaknesses of each player. Jack "The Shot" Cohen drafted me into my first league. My friend Jack was a terrific shooter, and he knew that I would set picks for him so he could get his shot off most any time. Jack was a pharmacist and part owner of a drug store. He lives in Florida. We're still friends. Bob Kanowitz was our best player and a scoring machine. He was a podiatrist who grew up in New York.

We won our first four games in a twelve-game schedule. It looked like we would make the playoffs. Then we lost six straight and wound up not making the playoffs. The next season, I was on a very good team with the Parlow brothers. We lost by three points in the final to a team that had beaten us three times before. In the last minute of the game, I was in position for a good shot from the corner, a shot I had made many times. Not that time. We got a smaller runner-up trophy, which they eventually stopped giving out.

Second never meant anything to me. Bruce Parlow, one of our best players, was a student of mine in 1963 when he was in eighth grade at Wilson Junior High School, the same one I had attended. I was a substitute teacher in his class at the age of 23 and had to leave school and serve two mandatory weeks in the Air Force Reserve. My stepdaughter, Sharon, is an art teacher now in Philadelphia and she taught there one year.

In 1982, I finally enjoyed being on a championship team. Our best player was Harvey Silverstein, who could really shoot. We won the final game of the season in overtime when Kenny Shapiro, our point guard, made seven out of eight foul shots to seal the deal.

Lee Mandel was the captain of my next two championship

teams. Lee is a criminal attorney in Philadelphia. When Susan was arrested for shoplifting, he was the first person I called. Lee took care of that mess just as he did when things began to get out of hand on the court, with confidence and no fuss. We had two top players, Wayne Rubinstein and Howard Fox, who kept us at a top level for two league seasons in a row. We lost during the regular season to a team we beat for our first championship.

To win a championship on any level, your top two players have to outplay the other team's best two players. I was generally a fourth or fifth pick, as long as I played my usual consistent game. That way, the outcome would not be altered.

My friend, Jerry Miller, was the captain of my next championship team. Bruce Parlow played an outstanding game, making 17 of 18 free throws, and we won the final.

Kenny Rotenberg picked me in a league shortly thereafter, and Jay Squarsky had a great game in the final. I was invited to Kenny's 40th birthday party and wrote a poem for the occasion.

Larry Levin and Arnie Aronovitz were on an over-40 team I fortunately played on, which also won a championship. We started out as one league for guys over 30. As everyone grew older, they added an over-40 league. I played on Tuesday and Thursday evenings in both leagues. I was always at least seven to ten years older than the people I played against, but I welcomed the challenge, even when it meant getting outrun and out-banged. Playing basketball always helped me keep myself together.

One year, I played for the championship on a Tuesday *and* Thursday in the same week, and we lost them both. Michael Goodman picked me on a memorable over-40 team. We won our next to last game to make the playoffs and lost the last game by 25 points. It looked like we had no chance, but we beat the #2 seeded team in the first playoff game. We beat the #1 ranked team in the second round and won the championship by beating the #3 team. Who needs rankings? Mike Goodman, our captain, played great. Norman Ginsberg, our #1 draft pick, played very well, too. He was an outstanding player at Olney High School and then played at Temple, where he backed up the great Guy Rodgers.

We had championship shirts made, which I wore a few times. The memory is the thing that counts, and I still cherish them.

B'nai Brith started a team in Lower Moreland. We won all our games. I was the eighth man on a nine-man team. I got a championship lightweight jacket. I only wore it a few times. Shelly Cardonick, Harvey Silverstein, Larry Levin, and Arnie Aronovitz were all on that team. My secret? Stay close to people with talent. That was the key to my non-talented life.

I must make one thing clear. Winning these championships was not because of me. I did my small part, avoided too many turnovers, played team ball, and always hustled. I guess those qualities are worth something, after all.

My friend, Barry Forman, who is now over 80 and still playing, picked me for his team in 1993. A team we lost to in the regular season couldn't touch us in the final. Barry made some big shots down the stretch, and I rebounded well.

That game remains meaningful for another reason. My cousin, Shelly Cardonick, was on the team. He was our #1 pick. He became sick with ALS and passed away. He was a great guy and a great competitor. We all remember him and miss him. His father, Ruby, was a great help to my father when he really needed it. These things take us beyond basketball, but the bonds we formed on the court left lasting impressions for many of us.

I was fortunate and had very few injuries over the years. One year, I walked in a swimming pool for three months to help heal a hamstring injury. My back was in pain many times, which is no doubt a result of going up against so many men who were simply bigger and stronger. I was gamer. Once I came to a playoff game partially bent over and could barely run, but I played, and we won.

I sold life insurance to some of my teammates, which was a win/win for all of us. Luckily, none of them died on the court and cashed in too soon.

I loved playing basketball. Going back to my earliest idols, I loved passing the ball and making people better. I had no problem being the fifth scoring option on a five-man team. I was a character actor, I guess, like the butler in those 1940s movies or the bad guy in cowboy flicks. I just wanted to show up and help my team win.

Winning was great. I loved all the guys and the camaraderie we formed. The chance to run and bang people and get banged back wore me out—in a good way. As a highly anxious person, it was the best medicine I could take.

That league played games once a week, and on Saturday afternoons we played half court. I grew up playing half court in the playgrounds, and I loved it. In many ways, it was more physical and demanding than playing full court. I could be a much more aggressive offensive player in half court games. In the league, I was a role player. I rebounded and defended big, tough players underneath the basket. I passed the ball well. I knew the game. I was physical and was not reluctant to bang and push people. Many people complained and said I fouled excessively. In thirty years playing in many leagues I only fouled out five times.

RICHARD G. KASSEN

A Tsunami Hits Philadelphia

WITH WORK IMPROVING and the status quo at home *seeming* to hold steady, things were going well heading into the 90s, but a domestic tsunami was about to hit. Susan was living a sad and tormented life. I always supported her. My parents, my sister, and even my kids had a hard time relating to her. I didn't leave her for anyone else. The whole process gave me no pleasure at all. We rarely argued when we were together. She was always supportive wherever and however she could. She had a major personality flaw, however, that could not be helped. My brother-in-law, Howard, who is a psychiatrist, told me that she could not be treated for what he called a borderline narcissistic personality.

Susan had a compulsive need to spend as little as possible. I believe in that, too—to a point—but I don't think I obsess over things like she did. For example, she would not go to a hairdresser. She would not take our youngest son to a barber. Instead, she went to a barber school because it was cheaper. When I would come back from the barber, she wanted me to return right away, so I could have more hair cut off. Got to get your money's worth.

She wanted to pass underwear down from each child to the next, and for a time she was successful with that idea. She collected coupons by the dozen and used them on unrelated items.

When I gave out nice, quality pens to clients who purchased policies from me, she called around to get the pens cheaper.

Susan never equated cost with quality. That was one flaw. When

229

I started doing better financially, her feelings never changed.

One day, she brought home 12 leather jackets for our sons to try on. They were made from thick, hard leather, and none of us boys liked them. They were inexpensive, but totally unattractive.

I could have had a continuous running argument with her over the extremes she went to with her frugality. I rarely did, because I just didn't have it in me to be so confrontational.

In every aspect of our lives, however, I tried to get her to appreciate quality. She never shopped for herself. At least she was consistent. There are many people in our country who are compulsive buyers. She was the opposite. We went to early bird dinners. We kept an entertainment book for discount restaurants. I must confess, I was a willing accomplice in many of these ventures and decisions, especially when it came to food.

Even today, I remain neurotic about over-spending. We all have personality flaws, but rational people can acknowledge them and try to change or modify their behavior. You can never totally change. Maybe a few can, but only a few.

Susan was a narcissist and incapable of empathy. That gene was simply missing. Living with someone like that is a problem. Unfortunately, the president of the United States has the same problem, but much worse. Fortunately for all of us, Susan did not suffer from delusions of grandeur.

One time, I was listening to rock music in my office. She came downstairs and shut it off without asking me.

"How can you listen to that shit?"

That was her only comment. Explaining to her that I liked listening to that music was a fruitless waste of time. She knew how important music was to me, but it made no difference.

I took my kids to the Spectrum to see Elton John, Billy Joel, and Neal Young, among others. I always had the radio playing while working in my basement office. *Forever Young* by Alphaville was an 80s favorite. Susan could never understand why I listened to rock and roll, and I just ran out of reasons to tell her. For me, that music makes me feel good. Is there really any other explanation needed? I guess narcissistic people have trouble accepting things outside of what matters to them. We all have different points of view, I guess. Some people love spicy food. Some don't. Some people love sports, while some don't. Susan's father had no interest in sports. She could never understand my passion for these games, as a player and a fan.

Respecting other people and their points of view is critical to functioning successfully in society, especially where it must begin with our most intimate relationships. It is difficult at times; that's for sure. Although I understand why so many people find the current president attractive, I have a hard time accepting him or his views. I see him as a con man. He is a great pitchman and has an uncanny knack for tapping into his followers' fears. Many people are happy because the stock market is up. I get it.

But I digress, which is easy to do in today's political climate.

After returning home from a business trip to Hong Kong, I went over to my friend's home to watch a 76er playoff game. We had no cable at home. My wife did not want us to spend money on things like cable TV. When I came back to the house, an obvious punishment was awaiting me. All my clothes had been put out on the porch, neatly of course. I had left home to watch the game and didn't realize Susan did not know I was gone.

Her reaction was shocking, but not surprising, I guess. Susan had a life of her own that I could never understand. For example, there was the time when my basketball buddy, Lee, saved her from getting in terrible trouble. She had gone shopping at a TJ Maxx with a friend. I later learned that they would switch more expensive items for cheaper ones. She got away with this, and I suppose it gave her some kind of psychological high. She certainly didn't need to do it. Perhaps you can call it a form of sickness.

Well, her luck ran out one day, when a store detective watched her do it all and caught her before she left. The police were called, and Susan was taken to the round house in Center City Philadelphia.

I got a call from the station late at night. I was already upset because she had been missing for quite some time and I hadn't heard from her. What a crazy thing, to find out that your wife was arrested for shoplifting! I called Lee, who said she would be forced to attend classes on the consequences of her actions on other unsuspecting people. I didn't think that would make any difference to her, because Susan didn't care about others—not in any genuine way—and that unfortunately included her whole family.

I drove down to the station at six a.m. the next morning. She had spent the night in jail and was not a happy camper.

Putting Life in Life Insurance

THE 80S BECAME A TURNAROUND DECADE for me. I finally found my passion and became ready to commit to doing whatever was necessary to achieve and be productive in my profession.

My focus was narrow. If it took working seven days a week, I was ready. Sports, music, and entertainment would have to come second. Even my family would have to be my secondary pursuit. I organized a small office in the basement of our home in Huntingdon Valley. I drove all over the surrounding counties and, when necessary, into New Jersey and Delaware. There was no GPS back then, so I had to get directions for every turn I was taking on those trips. At night, because street signs were hard to read, finding my destination could be challenging.

Up until that time, I had never made earning money a primary goal. I believed that if I just kept selling my wares, then the money would come.

Prospecting is the essential element necessary for achieving success when it comes to selling life insurance. People to call on is your inventory. I worked on straight commission. If an application was not approved and paid for, there was no sale. When an application was initially written, it was almost always accompanied by a medical exam. Sometimes, the applicant would fail the exam. The great basketball player, Magic Johnson, was found to have AIDS during a physical for life insurance. In many cases, doctors had to be contacted to obtain their records. Sometimes, we found notations of problems, which had never been mentioned by the

233

applicant. Many people have discovered medical problems first divulged by an insurance physical.

Years ago, I went to see *The Big Chill,* which was an excellent movie. Two of the friends in the story who had reconnected after many years were out one day in a small, two-man boat. One man asked the other what he was doing for a living.

"Estate planner," he said.

"Oh, you're a life insurance salesman," said the other.

I always remember that scene, even now, many years later. I had cards made up years ago that said "Insurance Consultant." For many years, I told people I was a life insurance broker. Now, when people ask me, I say I'm a life insurance salesman. It's akin to an uncontrollable drinker finally admitting to being an alcoholic.

I took a sociology course in college in 1959. The book listed all the occupations by prestige. Supreme Court justice was #1. Used car salesman was #100. Life insurance salesman was #99. My friend, Marc Levin, said why are you going to the Wharton school to become a life insurance salesman? It was not a bad question.

Many years ago, life insurance was sold by debit men. They would go door to door every week and collect premiums. Sometimes, the salesman would pocket the money. When a person died, the insurance would not be there.

My grandfather sold small policies to his large family. He sat in Horn & Hardart's restaurant every day, looking for prospects. My father was a general agent for Sun Life of America. All his policies were sold through that company. He had some sub-agents. He would get an override commission on anything they sold. During my early days in the business, I sold for Sun Life, too. After my breakdown in 1970, my life insurance sales became sparse for the next eight years. I worked as a reinsurance underwriter and later a manager, until I was fired in 1980 from PMA Insurance Company.

I have been told that selling life insurance is something that almost no one tries more than once in their lifetime. That's because when you fail, when you can't make it work, the emotional and psychological effects are so deep that it is something you never want to do again. I ran and ran. Every sale was a way of keeping away failure. Sales were like drugs. I needed a fix every day. I routinely wrote between 200 and 300 applications every year. Most great life insurance salesmen in this country believe in cash value and dividend-paying policies.

One year, I wrote 523 applications. Some of the applications never became policies. After leaving PMA, I met Shelly Blank, who owned Brokers Insurance Services. It turned out that most of my business was placed through his company, including term business with the lowest-cost companies we knew. I always believed in term insurance. Thankfully, I sold enough to qualify for a trip with Susan to Casa del Sol in Spain. This was a decade when I proved to myself that being passionate and dedicated to success was within my grasp.

There is a lot of failure in selling insurance, and you face a great deal of indifference. You are that squirrel in the backyard, scrambling around every day looking for food. I never really worried about or was affected by competing life insurance salesmen. My greatest concern was if the prospects I called on would spend money for my product. The other great competition remains with my own willingness to do all the things necessary to be successful. Fortunately, I have been able to maintain a fairly successful track record doing both.

Struggles at Home

AS OUR KIDS WERE GROWING UP, it would have been nice to initiate more family outings, but unfortunately, they were few and far between. We went to the movies in town on occasion to see films like *Chariots of Fire*, which we all liked, and *Risky Business*, which the boys loved, especially Tom Cruise in his breakout role.

Susan's outlook on spending money was depressing. This permeated our family plans for vacations, outing, and even birthdays. Her hang-up in this area kept many of those celebrations from being genuinely happy affairs.

Our big nights together involved going to Maggio's restaurant for their early-bird dinners. You had to get there before five p.m., but it was worth it, because you could get a full- course meal for $5.95. We went to Salvatore's on Street Road, too.

Susan was thrifty, to say the least. We kept an entertainment book. We went out on weekends only to restaurants that were in the books. We never spent more than $35 for a dinner. We rarely bought new clothes. My three sons wore hand-me-downs, even underwear. We lived a minimalist existence, surrounded by many neighbors who did not. Paul actually got some clothes that one of his friends no longer wanted. I am not proud of my complicity in this, but my sons survived.

Should I have taken my family out more?
Absolutely.
Should we have had more joyous times around birthdays?

Absolutely.
Should I forgive myself for trying to make things work?
Absolutely.

Susan only taught seven or eight piano students. She had no hobbies and no obvious purpose in life. By the time her boys were grown and pretty self-sufficient, she had no desire to go back to teaching full-time. I wish I could have channeled her back to teaching. Maybe she would have found a purpose in life and a genuine lust for living.

Once the boys were on their own, Susan and I effectively became housemates, with no intimacy or joint feeling to share our life together. She hated sports and rock and roll. She liked classical music, but never listened to it. When she got breast cancer, I stayed with her all the way. I was always loyal, no matter what.

Everything was about Susan, though, and how she saw life. She had no clue how her sons or I felt, nor did she care. She was consumed with trying to control everyone around her. For example, she had second thoughts about Josh going to medical school because it was expensive. She was very unhappy when he was accepted to study osteopathy instead of going to a traditional medical school. Her mother, Pauline, told her friends in Florida that Josh went to the University of Pennsylvania Medical School. She was ashamed that her grandson was at a school for osteopathy. She is the one who told Susan many years earlier to break off her engagement with her previous boyfriend. As a musician, whose economic future was in doubt, he was not suitable husband material. Susan ended up listening to her mother.

One evening, I was lying in bed when Susan came out of the bathroom. She looked at me and saw my anguish.

"If you ever leave me," she said, "I will pauperize you."

Her blazing eyes were revealing. I knew she was not kidding.

Luckily, the boys didn't get swept up too deeply in this drama.

Josh became friends with a female student whose name was Maria. She was Catholic. Susan liked the deal of Josh dating her as she was also on track to become a doctor. When I pointed out to Susan that Maria was Catholic, which I felt would prevent any serious future for them being together, Susan suggested that Maria could convert to Judaism. As a devout Catholic, I was sure that Maria would never convert. Susan had a blind spot for this, as empathy for others was somewhat lacking in her disposition.

Josh later met Teri Sklar, an occupational therapist who had graduated from Boston University. Her family lived nearby in Cheltenham. Susan felt that Josh was marrying beneath him economically, which cause some real animosity in the family. We went to the wedding at Ashbourne Country Club where Teri's father, Barry, was a member.

In spite of many tense and chilly moments at home, the boys have many fond memories of growing up under one roof. They still derive a great amount of pleasure recalling an incident that occurred at Josh's wedding when I was reciting the Motzi, a Hebrew blessing we say when we break bread before a meal. I did the Hebrew part just fine, but I got into trouble when I forgot the English translation. After a sentence or two, I just made something up about God and the bread. Seeing their father screw up always brought great joy to my sons, not in a nasty way, but in good fun.

Sadly, Susan rarely allowed herself to join in.

One time, she and I were having lunch in Willow Grove. She went on a rant about someone she was unhappy about because of something they had said to her. I tried explaining my point to Susan, that when you attack someone's point of view you should start off by saying, "In my opinion, what you're saying is incorrect." Most people make comments without having all the facts, and Susan was doing exactly that as were trying to eat. What she said in response to my comment was very chilling.

"Okay," she said, without missing a beat. "In my opinion, you are a fuckin' asshole."

It was quite embarrassing, as everyone in the restaurant could hear her.

Susan took no prisoners. One time in 1994, when our daughter-in-law was pregnant, she had a condition called eclampsia, which can be quite serious. She gave birth to our first grandchild, whose name is Sydney. I was sitting in the den when the call came from New York. Susan told Josh to leave his wife while he had the chance. She had been angry with Teri for something, and instead of being thrilled by the birth, she still couldn't get over her anger.

That conversation made something clear to me. I had to leave. I had always been loyal to Susan, through thick and thin, but I could not remain part of this madness any longer.

The problem was simple. How could I leave? All my files were in the house. If I tried to go, there was no telling what lengths Susan would go to. She could become violent, if need be. I was sure of that. In April of that year, I had an opportunity. Pauline, my mother-in-law, died, and Susan flew to Florida to retrieve her ashes. She was going to bring them back north for burial and take her father, Adolph, with her to live at home with us. She would be gone for one week, and I planned to pick them at the airport.

As soon as Susan left, I knew I had to make a move. I had one week. Leaving would be a monumental task, but I got it done. I found a place in the Cedarbrook Apartments on Limekiln Pike in Cheltenham Township. I found a mover and ordered telephone service. I used one of Josh's beds, as he was now gone, and his room was empty. I took care of all the details, but I had never fully appreciated how difficult the whole process would be.

Divorce is not cheap; that's for sure, especially when you consider lawyer costs, court hearings, and the ongoing harassment by Susan and her advocates. Neighbors and friends thought I was a bad guy for leaving her.

When her plane came in, I kept my word and picked up her and her father at the airport. She held her mother's ashes in an urn on her lap in the front seat. We drove into the garage. I took out their bags, and as they entered the house, I knew I had to get out of there. I said I was going out for gas.

I never came back. Susan called a friend of mine. He said maybe I was getting an oil change. When she went upstairs, Susan saw that my clothes were gone.

The battle was just starting. It was April 1995, and after almost 31 years of marriage, this amazing era of my life was over.

Rap

The 1980s, a decade of delusion,
The 1990s, a decade of confusion,
In your life, sorry for the intrusion,
To bring to you such an obvious conclusion.

The winds of change blow a mighty gust,
A world of AIDS and promiscuity,
We must temper our lust.

High unemployment — our living standards must adjust,
And intensely search for God, Truth —
And people we can trust.

My mother and her sister, my Aunt Lillian.

*Abraham Lincoln High School Hall of Achievement awards,
November 15, 1990, with (left to right) Dr. Russell Knorr, Robert K.
Abdullah, Esq., Barbara Ludman McMullen, John Schleyer,
me, and Dr. Harry Silcox.*

Team Y, over-40 basketball champions, 1998.

Accepting Jewish Basketball alumnae award, June 2014.

Josh, Adam, me and Bruce Drysdale, Lincoln H.S. and Temple University star basketball player at my awards banquet.

Josh's wedding, 1993, (left to right) Adam, Josh and Paul.

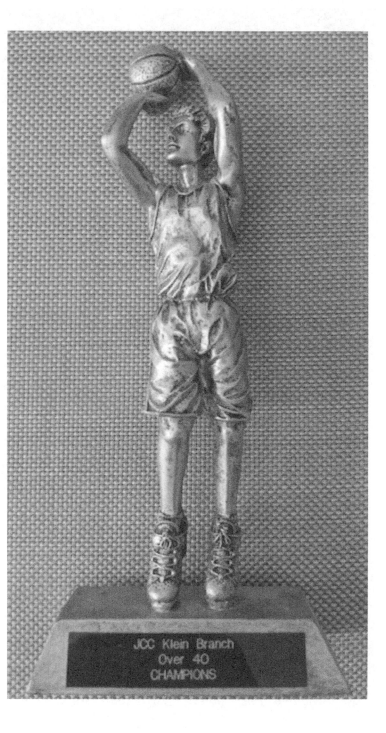

PART FOUR
Embracing Change

Moving On in Middle Age

MARRIAGE IS COMPLICATED. It's a physical, psychological, and highly emotional partnership. It also binds two people together by a legal contract. The odds of having a successful marriage are low. Everyone hopes that their marriage will defy the odds and work. Some men are afraid to commit in a relationship, which is understandable to me.

When things fall apart, for any reason, legal factors become a burden for both sides. In the process, behavior can become quote unpredictable and disturbing.

Marriage can be volatile. There are so many moving parts. In most cases, the most important factor is that men and women are different. I am not saying one sex is superior or inferior, just *different.* The next moving part is children, and the way they are raised can be a major issue for two parents, especially for those doing it for the first time.

Like with any sport of partnership, there are benefits and consequences. In businesses and professional partnerships, those involved may not always like each other, but they learn to get along because in the business world, the goal is to maximize revenue. A Gentile law firm hiring a Jewish partner is an example of putting aside differences for the betterment of the company. I had clients who were partners in all types of professions, and all of them had to learn to compromise. In the business world, it's probably easier to do that than people can manage inside a marriage.

One partner in that case may have to move in order to advance in their career. Does the other spouse go along and later become resentful? One spouse may want a dog. The other may not. They may differ politically. Sex for a woman may depend on her mood, while men are simply not too fussy. The presence of children may complicate that aspect of a marriage, and men (or women) may come to feel abandoned emotionally. Over time, unspoken conflicts and resentments can build up for both parties.

All of this leads to change, and for someone middle-aged who is also an empty-nester, it's not always easy to navigate how this transpires. I spent several years trying to find my way through this lonely minefield.

The Price We Pay

SUSAN DID NOT WANT THE DIVORCE. She called me repeatedly during the first six months after I left and organized mutual acquaintances to call me day and night. She came to my apartment, where she was met by security people in front of the building, who told her she could not enter. One time, she bolted by them and banged on my apartment door for a long time before leaving.

The cost of the divorce was quite substantial. Fighting with my estranged wife to hold on to a fair share of my assets was time-consuming and expensive. The process took five years. Susan did not come to an agreement easily. She had three lawyers and hired a forensic accountant to ferret out all future commissions I was due.

I hired a female attorney on the recommendation of a friend. She led me to believe she would accomplish certain things, which proved to be false. She was totally ineffective, and I replaced her.

The master who heard my case in Norristown recommended a female attorney from a different firm. She was low key, but effective. I was forced to go to court on at least four occasions. I had to hire my accountant to bring documents that proved I was not hiding money.

The divorce took a toll on us both, financially and emotionally, and we eventually settled. I thought the deal was more than fair. I was free. There were no small children involved. I know that people who go through a divorce with young kids have it much worse. We were relatively lucky in that respect, even though the divorce was not a welcome change for our three boys.

The baggage each person brings into a relationship is rarely seen. It wasn't for me. I didn't know Susan had been beaten as a child. I wasn't initially aware of her deep narcissism and need for control. I thought I was marrying an attractive Jewish woman who lived five blocks from my home. I don't regret marrying Susan for one second. She gave birth to our three wonderful sons, who produced my four terrific grandchildren.

I was loyal to Susan throughout our marriage, and if I hadn't felt forced to flee, I would have gone the distance. When you are married to someone for thirty years, the time you spent together can never be diminished or erased.

A successful marriage needs two people committed to making it healthy and keeping it that way through thick and thin. That's much easier said than done, but it's essential to keep things going in a good way.

I just watched a television series on the Discovery Channel called *Genius*. The geniuses were Einstein and Picasso. In each instance, their spouses were sacrificed for their work. The women were drawn to both men because being in the company of a genius is a powerful aphrodisiac. However, those women paid an emotional price to reap the rewards of being so close to a genius.

Long ago, I read a book called *What Makes Sammy Run*. A woman named Madeline Fox had sex with Sammy. When she was asked why, she said, "I wanted all that ambition inside me."

People come together sometimes for strange reasons. These days, they meet through dating sites. There are tough questions each person should ask on that first meeting, especially if either of them wants to save time. Why waste your valuable time with a person you are not meant to be with? Time is a finite resource and learning to use it well is essential. This applies to our relationships, too, and it certainly did for me in my choice to get divorced.

To complicate matters, Susan and I were victims of a Ponzi scheme, which began a year before I left home. My stockbroker had recommended a company called Bennett Funding, located in

Syracuse, New York. I was looking for interest returns, and they were marketing U.S. government agencies that were looking for loans. The interest rate was two percent higher than the market. I was assured it was safe and legitimate. An insurance company checked their books and guaranteed it to a degree.

The checks came in on time until they didn't. We lost a considerable sum of money. The courts appointed a man to go after all the assets and possible money owed to the certificate holders. We ended up getting back about 47 percent of what we had put in.

It was a painful experience. Sadly, we have seen much worse since then. When the Madoff scandal became news, I sympathized with the victims. At the time, when the money is rolling in, you kind of feel like a greedy fool. In essence, that is exactly what you are. We all hate to do dumb things, such as being victimized by a Ponzi scheme. We all make mistakes on this journey, and we try to learn from them. They call it being human. Sometimes, failure has made me feel *too* human.

During the years of the divorce process, I received envelopes from my attorney every month with each and every minute itemized. I feel for all people who have gone through this process, and there have been many. I grew exhausted from all the litigation, and Susan became tired of facing endless lawyer bills. Finally, we came to an agreement, which was not easy.

RICHARD G. KRASSEN

Serendipity

I DATED FOR TWO-AND-A-HALF YEARS following my separation from Susan. Once I put a personal ad in *The Jewish Exponent;* I met women from various walks of life. In November 1997, I got a response from a woman named Carole.

"I'm dating someone," I told her, "and when that ends, I will contact you. One woman at a time is all I can handle."

She was very impressed by me calling her back and leaving that message. I called her again in early December.

"Let's meet at Murray's Delicatessen in Rydal."

She said she didn't like that place, so we settled on Rembrandt's in the Fairmount section of Philadelphia. Carole lived in Melrose Park, a few miles from my apartment. I liked that she lived close by. It would mean lower gas costs and less travel time.

We learned that we both had attended Penn and had graduated together in 1962. Carole was a political science major. We never had any classes together, but we knew a lot of the same people. She took out our yearbook and saw my picture.

That was December 14th, the same day as Paul's birthday. He turned 26 years old on the day I met Carole.

I told her when she got in the car that I would never live with anyone or marry again. She said she wanted to marry again. We kept driving to the restaurant and had brunch. A trio played romantic classical music.

255

After we left, we went to Kelly Drive. It was a beautiful sunny day. The air was crisp. The rest is history.

Shortly after we met, Carole came to the gym to see me play basketball in a series of over-50 playoff games. It was so nice to have Carole there at every game, rooting for us. She may have been our good luck charm, because we won the championship.

Carole and I did many nice things together. She was always patient. The first time we went to the Wissahicken to hike was on New Year's Day, 1998. I went to REI and bought a pair of hiking shoes. It must have been the coldest day of the year, and that just exacerbated my troubles, as some of the inclines were major, at least for me. I kept asking her how much longer. She was very annoyed with my repetitive questions, as I had little interest in continuing to freeze, except for the fact that I enjoyed her company so much

Carole is the last woman I ever dated. This led to a deeper commitment, and we bought a house together in Cheltenham in 2000. The address was 1117 Ashbourne Road. My birthday is 11-17, which was a nice coincidence. Martin Scorsese, Danny Devito, Gordon Lightfoot, and the iconic New York Met, Tom Seaver, are among many others sharing that birthday.

The Ashbourne Country Club was across the street. Every morning, I found golf balls on our front lawn. Our handyman once had his front windshield broken by an errant golf ball. The club watered their grass every morning, which created a beautiful effect. The club, which had a good reputation, was predominantly Jewish, which actually became a problem because as the older members died, their sons and daughters left the neighborhood, many after graduating from college. As a result, the club closed down shortly after we moved in and became overrun with tall grass and weeds.

Our home was a nice two-story colonial, all brick and stone, with a large front walk and a generous backyard, complete with a rock garden. It was well-located, just 35 minutes from Center City.

Life was good. Still, even though I had said I would never get married again I changed my mind. Life was that good with Carole. We took our vows on a beautiful October day in 2004, in a lovely venue near Rittenhouse Square. It was a beautiful family time. My grandson, Eli, was born eleven days after the wedding.

Why did I change my mind? We had been together for almost seven-and-a-half years. I was growing tired of explaining our relationship. I was ready—as ready as any man ever is.

Around 2010, Carole decided that she wanted to live in Center City, but I refused. We liked our home in Cheltenham, and while she wanted a change, I held fast to staying put. I liked the privacy and space our home provided. Paying higher taxes in the city of Philadelphia, as well as paying to park my car, did not appeal to me.

We fixed up our house and committed to stay. There were several issues to address, but we were fine with that. For example, we had mold in our basement after several bouts of leaking water. This caused a great amount of clutter, and we finally had to hire a company to remove the mold and waterproof the basement.

There was a bigger problem outside our home. Every winter, there would be snow. Many years there would be ice. It was my responsibility to find someone to shovel our substantial front walk. It had to be cleared within 24 hours of any fresh snow, so that people passing by would not fall down and get hurt. It was difficult to find steady people to help us. Many times, during lighter snow falls, I would shovel.

By the winter of 2014, after struggling with yet another season of shoveling snow and breaking up ice, I had seen enough. No one was willing to clear away ice after eight p.m., however, so it was left up to me. I had to do it, because if a child fell the next morning on his or her way to school, I could have been sued.

One night, I was outside chopping ice in a howling wind. The temperature was way below freezing. The ice was not breaking up. I used special granules to melt it, but it was simply too cold to do the trick. After two hours of back-breaking work, I came into the house, my hands and feet numb as could be, waving a white flag. It was actually a white handkerchief full of cold phlegm.

"Carole, I surrender!" I said. "Let's move to Center City."

I was 74 years old. I did not want to die face down in my driveway and miss my 75th birthday party.

As many people know, moving from a home into an apartment is a costly, time-consuming venture. First, we had to sell our home for a decent price. My friend, Jeff Parkins, was our real estate broker. He had significant problems trying to do his job. The school system in Cheltenham was not considered on a par with surrounding districts. The property taxes were high. There was little commercial property in Cheltenham. Instead, there were many churches and synagogues, which paid no taxes at all.

We got lucky. The couple who bought our house had two older children. One was working at Einstein Hospital and one was a student at Temple. Both institutions were within 15 to 20 minutes by train or car. The taxes did not scare them away, so we made a deal on a fair price for everyone.

I took a chance prior to the sale. We engaged a mortgage broker to help us find options on a rental property. Buying a condo buy at age 75 was not a consideration. We looked at quite a few places. There was only one we both liked: the St. James, a 45-story apartment building, overlooking Washington Square.

The unit we liked had carpeting, but we wanted hardwood floors. Nancy, who worked for the leasing company, called me to say an apartment with our preferred flooring was available on the 19th floor, with a floor-to-ceiling view of Washington Square and the Delaware River. We went down and signed the lease before our house had sold. We took a chance and it all worked out.

We moved in May 2015. I had always said I would never move into Center City Philadelphia, but I loved living in town from the first day. I liked the energy and the feeling of being alive in that urban setting. The diversity was stimulating. Two professional basketball players from the 76ers lived in the building. A 76er coach, too. The building has an indoor pool and a good workout room. The parking lot is attached to the apartment house, which is especially good in the winter. We only have one car now. Whenever possible, we walk. I walk outside two to three miles every day, as long as the weather permits. I don't use the pool or the workout rooms because I prefer being outdoors, probably because I spent so much time outside when I was a kid.

Such a big change was not as hard as I thought it would be, not by a long shot. But I'm not always so easy to welcome new things. I'm embarrassed to report that in December of 2015, I still owned a flip phone. This became highlighted when my grandsons, Miles and Eli, slept over in our second bedroom during the holidays.

One day, my phone fell into the pool. Eli rescued it, and we put it in a bowl of brown rice. We waited a few days to see if that trick would work to dry it out, but it was dead. I went out and purchased a Samsung 5 and have loved it ever since.

This is my life. I personify resistance to change until I am forced to adapt, and I end up happy. This has happened repeatedly, with big and small things. Leaving my wife, departing our home, and even getting a new phone. Each move requires a willingness to change or a damn good reason to do so!

Love of the Game

I SURELY LOVE CAROLE, but I love basketball, too—always have. For many years, I was able to manage both, until my body just couldn't keep up—with basketball.

Back in the day, when Carole first came to my games, we had a few notable players on our team. Dr. Elliot Gevis was our captain and point guard. He had many injuries, but he healed quickly and kept playing. He picked a very good team. Elliot was a great guy. I always knew that if I became sick, even in the middle of the night, I could call him, and he would be at my side in no time. He would've done that for anyone. That's just who he was. He had an excellent shot and battled anyone he was guarding.

Dr. Harris Mann was our center. He was the nicest man you could ever meet. He was a dentist, and his patients adored him. He always asked about them and their families in a very sincere way. He and his wife, Maxine, are wonderful people and excellent parents to their daughters.

The competition was wonderful. At the end of each game, we all shook hands, as everyone in the league were friends. Most of us had played together on the same team at one time or another. I was lucky because getting injured was always a possibility, and I avoided anything serious. I broke different fingers and had back problems from time to time, but I was never out of action for too long.

The game of basketball provided an emotional release of energy for me, and the exhaustion I felt at the end of most games was more than welcome.

The game is different now. It is less physical, and with the three-point shot becoming so big, the game is more guard-oriented. The old days of dominant centers are gone. In fact, more and more of them are launching threes like foul shots. I welcome these changes, as they're fun to watch, but I do miss the good old days of banging and bruising under the boards.

Over all my years of playing basketball, from age ten to age 72, I was very fortunate to be part of 14 championships as a player and one as a coach. Nine times I played in a final game and lost. Once, I coached a final and lost at the buzzer. Twenty-five finals. Those losses were much more painful than the joy of winning.

Lessons from My Mother

MY MOTHER WAS ALWAYS AN INDEPENDENT WOMAN. She took care of her own affairs and was never needy. She used to balance her own checkbook and all her finances, and she bought her own CDs from the bank right up through age 90. Finally, she started asking me to handle her savings and to routinely change them. I still remember buying her CDs and trying to get her certain percentage points on the interest.

She called me once during that time to complain.

"You only got me such and such percent," she said. "I see in the paper there's a bank in Wyoming that could have given me another three tenths of a percent, so why didn't you connect me with them?"

"Mom, next CD you want I'm not going to do it for you. You're going to call the bank in Wyoming and handle it yourself."

"Forget about it," she said.

Her generation grew up managing every penny. This was not a negative, though, because she always paid attention, even into her 90s. But when she wanted me to spend half an hour on the phone with some bank in Wyoming, I said no! Morgan Stanley would be fine right here at home, even with three tenths less of a percent.

My mother could be a real pill when she chose to speak her mind in no uncertain terms. For example, she would look at her great-granddaughter and say, "Look, you're getting heavy. You should really be careful with what you eat." Everybody would object and wonder aloud how she could say such an awful thing.

"That's a nasty thing to say, Mom," I'd tell her.

She'd shrug and dismiss my objection. That's just who my mother was, for better or for worse. If she saw something she didn't approve of, she usually had a set reaction.

"What the hell are you doing?"

She was rarely nuanced about her feelings. On the other hand, the nicest thing about my mother was that she gave me so much freedom when I was growing up. Today, many parents give their children a tremendous amount of attention, which is wonderful at first glance, but to my mind that kind of focus can be good *and* bad.

My mother gave me an incredible amount of latitude. I was able to live my life as I saw fit. The downside was that although all my other friends, mostly Jewish, had career paths to be a dentist, a doctor, or an accountant, nothing was ever discussed in my house about these aspirations.

One night, my parents got into a big argument while I was in bed. They were bickering about what I was going to do with my life after I got out of school, because at the time it remained a big question mark. I overheard their thoughts as they grew louder.

"He can do the insurance business with me," my father said.

"Richard is not a salesman," said my mother. "He doesn't like small talk; he's not a back slapper, and he's not particularly aggressive with people. He just doesn't have any of the traits that you really need to be a salesman."

I was in college at the time and I have to admit my mother was right. Eventually, I evolved to have a little more confidence and assertiveness, but at the time I had no goals or vision. I must say that even as I drifted during the years following college, the stern, no-nonsense approach of my mother laid the groundwork for me to become much more disciplined and focused as I grew older.

My Sister Ellen

FOR REASONS I CAN'T EXPLAIN, I had a minimal relationship with my sister while we were growing up. She was more than five years younger than me, and we never had any conversations I can remember. I pretty much considered myself an only child. Looking back, I don't feel good about that, but it's just the way it was.

Ellen had a stormy relationship with our mother because she wanted more from her than my mother would give. My mother, being a sixth child out of eight, always felt that she had been neglected. Instead of using that experience to change how she communicated with her own daughter, she carried over that behavior into her own household.

"I was neglected. Period. That's the way I was treated, so I'm going to do the same thing with my kids. I felt the pain so I'm going let them feel it, too."

As if it were our fault?

Unfortunately, my sister grew up in an ongoing confrontational relationship with our mother. Ellen wanted the normal things a child needs and wants from a mother: attention, dialogue, meaningful time, and fun experiences. Mother didn't really understand this, and left Ellen alone to much of the time.

Ellen's Sweet 16 party at the George Washington Motor Lodge was a fun event. She had plenty of cute girlfriends, but they were five years younger than me and at the time, which was an eternity. She told me that one of the girls always wanted to come over to the house because she wanted to be there when I got home from school. Too bad I was out of their age range and couldn't capitalize on the availability of so many nice girls.

Later, when I married my first wife, she and my sister didn't get along at all, which meant I had an even more limited relationship with Ellen. It was only after I left Susan that I began to develop a real relationship with my sister. Now we're pretty close. We talk at least once a week. It's much better, and I am grateful for that.

Ellen spent much of her career helping children improve their reading and writing skills. Many young men and woman who have graduated from prestigious colleges are greatly indebted to Ellen for her work with them. I am very proud of my sister.

Fresh Air

IF SOMEONE ASKED ME who I would like to hang out with for 90 minutes—more than anyone else in the world—my answer would not be Charles Barkley, Bill Russell, or Hank Aaron. While they are iconic sports legends, the person I would choose is Terry Gross. She is a treasure, locally, nationally, and probably all over the world.

Ms. Gross is possibly the best interviewer I've ever heard on radio, in particular on National Public Radio (NPR). She has been interviewing people on her show since 1975. While I only began listening to NPR in 2000 (thanks to my wife, Carole), the experience of doing so has elevated the last 18 years of my life in many unexpected and very welcome ways. For example, many of her guests came from humble beginnings and faced adversity many times in their life. Yet they still rose above the obstacles to reach notable achievements.

I never thought I had the wherewithal to write this book. After years of hesitating, I finally realized I could do whatever was necessary to achieve this dream. A friend warned me that no one outside my family and a few friends would find my book worth reading. Okay. I'm not famous. But neither were the people on Terry's show at one time. I will be dead and gone soon, and I want all of my life's layers laid bare.

Terry does the same thing with all of her guests in their interviews. She makes them all feel important and creates an environment in which she can be trusted as a person to whom they can speak openly and honestly. I would be thrilled to hang out with Terry Gross, which I hope might someday be possible.

Terry's manner on the air and her modulating voice allow her guests a feeling of ease and control. She asks excellent, penetrating questions, which allows her subject to be the main focus of the interview, instead of herself. I don't believe she is perceived to have strong political biases, but some may dispute that. In fact, I have heard that a few people have walked out of her show, albeit rarely.

For me, a sports talk radio enthusiast for my entire life, Terry Gross has opened up a universe of new ideas and perspectives, and I have a ton of questions I would love to pose to her. I'd begin with her upbringing in Brooklyn, New York. Did she know Larry David, the great comedian, or Rico Petrocelli, the former shortstop of the Boston Red Sox, or the comic Elayne Boosler, who all went to her high school? I think the school has closed by now, and I wonder how she feels about that, too.

I'm curious about who her favorite interview was and what made that particular person stand out. That must be a tough question, as so many wonderful, interesting, entertaining and even controversial people have been on her show. I'd like to know why she believes people walked off her show and what her thoughts are about that.

Terry Gross attended the University of Buffalo, and I'm curious about why she chose that school.

I know we have something special in common. Both of us took time off to travel during or after college. I did mine after graduating, and Terry took a year off during her studies, which was a gutsy thing to do back then, especially for a young woman. She did her travels with the young man she married. I'd like to know where they went, if they saw the same sights as I did on my trip, and what meaning and influence that has had on her life.

I wonder why she came to Philadelphia and how she became involved in public radio. How did she start doing interviews and how did she become such a master? Why is the show named *Fresh Air*?

I know Terry appreciates movies and music, and I'd like to ask her about one of my favorite movies, *Twelve Angry Men*. It made me feel hopeful to see how these 12 strangers started out with major disagreements and finally came together to make a unanimous decision. Lee J. Cobb and Henry Fonda headed up a great cast. I'd love to know the answers to at least some of these questions.

I love biographies, autobiographies, and memoirs. I enjoy talking to strangers and asking them questions about their life. Most people's lives are compelling and interesting in one way or another, if only we are curious enough to find out.

Terry Gross knows this because she is genuinely interested in people, as well as being interesting herself, and she knows how to find out what makes others captivating. She does her homework, is always engaging, and is respected by people all over the country.

Seriously, Terry Gross is a rock star to me. Meeting her at some point would really make my day!

Listening to her over all these years has taught me to identify my own thoughts and feelings in a more clear and concise way.

I remember that sixth grade student who was afraid to go to the blackboard because he might have the wrong answer. All I can say is, thanks to Terry Gross, I am at the blackboard now. Anytime she's ready, I'm holding a spot for her on a nearby park bench.

Memories of Ann

I RECENTLY HAD THE PLEASURE of speaking to Ann Karchin's youngest brother, Paul, who is a professor at Wayne State University. We had a nice conversation, and he told me that when his mother died, he found a lot of memorabilia, including pictures of Ann. One in particular shows her as a ballerina at the age of eight, when she had aspirations to become a professional dancer.

This conversation brought back extremely strong memories for me, because when you are eight or nine years old and see someone your own age die, it is a frightening experience that sticks with you forever. You simply don't think at that age that anyone, including yourself, can die, much less so soon.

The opportunity to speak with Ann's brothers has been gratifying. They probably would not have been born if Ann had not passed so young. Now, they both have families of their own. Paul's daughter is a violinist in New York and teaching music.

My short connection with Ann remains as a pivotal piece of my life. Many people must look back to their childhood and remember a friend they were close to who either disappeared or even died growing up. All of us are probably still pained by those experiences, and I feel it's important to honor their memory.

My Three Sons

JOSH, ADAM, AND PAUL have left indelible marks on my life. As I look back, certain particular events stand out with each of them, all memorable for different reasons.

When Josh was a senior in high school, his friend Billy Swotes came over to our home to play chess. Josh agreed to drive Billy home in his brown Chevy Nova, a solid car with a six-cylinder engine. There were lighter weight cars at that time, which got much better gas mileage, but where safety was concerned, I preferred my son driving a heavier, more secure automobile. I am very frugal, but not when it comes to the welfare of my children.

Billy lived a few miles away. Josh didn't come back for a while, but I wasn't concerned because I thought they were at Billy's home. Then the phone rang.

"Hello, this is Officer Watson," a voice said. "Your son has been in automobile accident."

My first instinct was just like any parent's.

"Is he all right?"

"Sir, all I can tell you is to go to Warminster General Hospital."

Susan and I were terribly upset. As some people know, your mind can go to bad places when you hear news like this and don't know any more details. When we arrived at the hospital, we scrambled to find him. Thank God he was alive and without any severe injuries. He had a broken nose and internal injuries, but nothing that didn't heal just fine in time. Billy ended up in a different hospital, which treated non-serious injuries.

We were all lucky. Many kids and parents are not. We were spared what could have been, but still were quite shaken by what did go down that night. The accident had occurred so close to our home. The other car was driven by a man named Beerly. He crossed the yellow line and hit our car head on. They found beer bottles in the man's back seat. I presume he had been drinking.

Thank God for that heavy Chevy.

When Josh was ready to apply for college, we discussed long-range career plans and his goal of becoming a doctor. Josh had never indicated this desire before, but his mother and I thought he surely had the potential. He had done quite well in chemistry and math, two important subjects to excel in for a medical career.

I must admit I was very authoritative in choosing where he would go, and after considering many possibilities, I decided that Ursinus College would be the best fit for him and a good choice for us. They had an excellent chemistry department and were considered a very fine pre-med school. Back in 1983, the cost to go there was reasonable. In fact, the year after Josh enrolled, a magazine came out with a "Best Value Education" feature and Ursinus was listed in the top 10 of all colleges in the country!

Josh enjoyed Ursinus and was elected president of the student body in his senior year. His four-year grade point average was good, but not great, just like in high school. Josh loved to party; like most college kids, having fun was important to him. When he ran for president, his female opponent wanted to eliminate drinking on campus. He was all for it, though, and not shy about saying so, and of course this helped him win the election.

Josh applied to many medical schools, which all rejected him. His GPA was just not high enough among all of the competition. Somehow, a grade point average was the gold standard for admittance. Fortunately, he found a perfect fit close to home, a school that happily wanted him and would provide solid medical training. The Philadelphia School of Osteopathic Medicine preferred applicants with more all-around experience. Being president of his class in college was a big plus in their eyes.

Josh is a doer, not a book grinder. He finds studying somewhat boring. He will always be a quick learner, but he's not cut out to be an academic. He graduated osteopathic school near the bottom quarter of his class, but he graduated, which is not that easy to do!

I remember a weeknight when Josh wanted to go to a party.

"Josh, you were out over the whole weekend," I said. "You need to study."

"Is there a limit on having fun, Dad?" he said. "Something they forgot to explain in the college handbook?"

After graduation, Josh did intern rotations on an Indian Reservation, at a Colorado ski lift center, and at other diverse venues. He was graded on his work in those places and always got an A. For him, doing was fun, and he did that well. He was thinking of a specialty to pursue. At the time, his grandmother was being treated in a physical rehab facility, so rehab medicine became attractive to him. He spent some time at Moss Rehab, where his great Aunt Esther was being treated. Teri Sklar, who was to become Josh's wife, was working there at the time as an occupational therapist after graduating from Boston University. Aunt Esther introduced them.

Josh was matched for his residency at Mt. Sinai Rehabilitation Hospital in New York City, where he received great training. One of his notable patients was Dennis Byrd, a football player from the New York Jets. He had become paralyzed in a collision with a teammate. After sustained effort by Mr. Byrd and his doctors, he was finally able to walk again. He made a speech, thanking God for his recovery. I'm so glad he was able to walk again, but I must say that God wasn't one of his doctors at Mount Sinai.

Adam was a good student, but like Josh, I never pushed him. He had a few good friends. Josh was much more gregarious and had many friends, but Adam did just fine.

When it was time to choose a college, he acted on his desire to be in a warm climate far from his mother. Her treatment of him growing up had been less than acceptable. For example, he took piano lessons three miles away from where we lived. Susan would forget to pick him up to bring him home.

Allowing an eight-year-old child to walk home by himself down the busy Industrial Highway was not good. Sometimes, she agreed to pick him up from school and arrived 30 minutes late. When he greeted her with a forlorn look, she would mock him. She called Adam her sensitive one, based on the visual dissatisfaction she saw him display as a result of her emotional abuse.

Susan and I went to see the counselor at the high school to explore which schools in Florida might be a good choice. This was 1986, toward the beginning of Adam's senior year in high school. The school we found most appealing was the University of South Florida, in Tampa. It was reasonably priced. He had the grades to get accepted. My uncle Jack taught economics there, but Adam did not need his help to qualify for admittance.

Strangely, my uncle was quite upset when he heard from my mother, his sister, that Adam had been accepted. He thought Adam used his name to help gain admission. I told him the facts. Adam said he had an uncle who teaches at the school, but he never referred to him by name, which was Jack Donis. I told my uncle that Adam was more than qualified.

My cousin, Jim, Jack's son, ran off to live in Venice, Italy after he graduated from NYU. They didn't get along. At that time, the University of South Florida did not have a football team, and the school existed under the national radar. Things sure have changed. Many people want to go there now, and the costs have shot up.

Adam became a Florida resident after year one. While the tuition was very affordable, he delivered pizza to pick up extra money. I bought him a used Chevy, which rarely needed repairs. Adam majored in accounting because I told him to. Otherwise, he had no particular interest in a major. He stayed five years and earned an accounting degree, which he had no intention of using in any professional capacity. I still thought that the mental challenges that the courses presented would serve him well.

Adam and Chris, his girlfriend, ran off and eloped. Susan was not happy. Chris was not Jewish, and Susan had no time or inclination to offer her approval. Chris and Adam came back to live in Pennsylvania, where Adam got a job selling fitness equipment. He loved working out and had a passion for the products. They initially lived in an apartment near us. Susan wanted Chris to convert to Judaism. We were not a religious family, although all three boys had their own Bar Mitzvah ceremony.

Adam and Chris eventually moved into a new house they bought in Coatesville, Pennsylvania, which was far away from us. Chris was a very nice woman. However, she wanted things from the marriage that Adam was not prepared to give, so she left him and found someone new. It happens. We hope she is happy.

Her father bought a life insurance policy from me. A few years after the divorce, I called him regarding his policy, and he screamed at me over the phone. I was an innocent party. He later apologized through his daughter and Adam, which was a convoluted process, but I understood it at the time. He liked Adam and was frustrated by their divorce. Welcome to the club.

Paul fought with his mother at times. She was tough on him, and he responded once by knocking over a full quart of milk.

Paul sold candy on the way home from school. He was a hustler at a young age, and I knew he would be fine. Back then, when the boys helped me with the lawn, I rewarded them with a giant Slurpee from 7-11.

I never worried about his grades. They weren't great, but they were acceptable, just like those of his two older brothers. Paul applied to Temple and was accepted into their music program. Susan wanted him to major in business, but I stepped in, as I wanted him to major in what he loved.

"He has skills," I said, "and will be fine."

After a year at Temple, Paul made a tape of his piano playing. He said he wanted to send it to William Patterson College, where they had a great jazz department headed up by Rufus Reed. They had great teachers and hand-picked their students. Fortunately for Paul, they had openings for piano players.

When Paul got there, he realized it would take maximum effort to survive and graduate. Many did not. As a rule, Paul practiced into the wee hours of the morning. His tenacity and drive got him through. There was no average in that program. You played in a group with other great players, which meant you had better perform at a top level. There was no hiding. You were there for everybody to see and hear. You'd better be a player.

Paul had to take some liberal arts courses. He took a history class in a large lecture hall, where the students all took notes.

That was the motto: Learn. Get good grades. Find a job.

One day, the teacher claimed that the Holocaust never occurred. None of students spoke up. They were not there to think critically or question authority, but strictly to get good grades. Suddenly, one student did stand up to challenge the professor.

"You can't make those statements," he said. "You are doing harm to all of us in this class. There is documented proof that you are giving false information."

That student's name was Paul Krassen.

I called my friend at B'nai Brith, who contacted the Jewish Anti-Defamation League. Paul's name appeared later in a story in *The New York Times*, which made me very proud.

Adam has successfully sold BMW 's and fitness equipment and he had a less than successful run at selling commercial real estate. Six years ago, someone suggested he sell medical supplement plans for people on Medicare. He now has more than a thousand clients and is considered an expert in the field. He combines making a great living with doing good service for people. For me, that is hitting the lottery. He has also become an outstanding referee for boys' and girls' lacrosse, soccer and basketball.

Paul has become successful at his own business, which he conducts by himself out of his home. His real love is playing jazz piano and he will soon be putting out a record. He bought a brand new Steinway piano because the quality of the sound is that important to him.

Josh is a physiatrist in a sports medicine group in Lehigh Valley. He loves to attend rock concerts and professional sports games.

There are many billionaires in the world. I am richer than all of them. In fact, I have spent five decades brimming with pride because of my three sons, and I hope they know how much joy and pleasure they have provided for me.

RICHARD G. KRASSEN

The Hall of Achievement

IN 1990, I RECEIVED THE HONOR of being placed into the Hall of Achievement at my alma mater, Lincoln High School, which is reserved for their most distinguished graduates.

Mr. Harry Silcox, my basketball coach, and I had become friendly when I was a substitute teacher there, and he recommended that I submit my resume for consideration. I had never thought about being included there, that I deserved such a distinction. But Coach pushed me to do it, so I did, and for some reason, they accepted me. I was proud to tell my kids and my coworkers, and everyone close to me was in attendance for the public event.

I was especially excited to share the news with my mother.

"Mom, I'm being put into the Hall of Achievement at my old high school."

Even I was surprised by her response.

She had already made arrangements to drive to Florida. Instead of leaving on a Tuesday, she would have had to change her trip to that Wednesday. My mother, however, did not want to disturb the plans she had already made. She didn't want to call her driver and do anything different, so she never went.

"If you were being put into the Hall of Achievement at Penn, I might go. But since it's only high school, I won't do it."

That was my mother. I was a grown man, of course, but when these honors come along, they can bring you emotionally back to your childhood days of wanting to please your parents in the worst way. I looked around and saw quite a few parents of those being honored. My father had passed away, so with my mother opting to be in Florida, I had no parents. My mother simply would not change her departure day, not even for something that meant so much to her son. That remained very painful to me because she put her own convenience ahead of going to the trouble of sharing this honor with me and our family.

She didn't want to experience the joy of her son being recognized. It was more important to keep her schedule. Losing that trophy when I was a kid, when she let it get away, was nothing compared to this. That was just a stupid little glitch in life. On the other hand, this was something very hard to accept. My father always showed up to my basketball games, and I knew he would have been there with me, come hell or high water. In fact, if he had been alive, both of them would have been there. He would have made sure of that, despite any protest from my mother.

Anyway, we had a great night at my old school and enjoyed basking in the momentary adulation — all part of feeling that it's been a life well lived.

My Personal Hall of Fame

IN 2012, I RETIRED FROM PLAYING BASKETBALL. During my last pick-up game on a Sunday morning, Bruce Jaffe, chased me around the gym for fouling him in an overzealous manner. Bruce is 6'4" and weighed about 300 pounds at the time. He liked to post up as close to the basket as possible, so moving him off the block was essential. I was giving away about three inches and 90 pounds. Bruce is also about 20 years younger than me, too.

Friendships are largely abandoned while you are playing against them on another team. Pleasing your teammates is all that matters. If I didn't play defense, they wouldn't have let me in the gym. I was usually the fifth offensive option on my team, a distinction well earned. In pick-up games, if the man guarding me was someone I could dominate, I asked for the ball. On some days, I was effective.

My friend, Jerry Kasner, was a defensive player, too. He was a fine team player and both of us functioned best as role players, surrounded by scorers and shooters.

I first contemplated retiring from basketball in 2005, when I turned 65. Norty Levine urged me to continue playing. During the next seven years, my team went to the finals four times. We won the first two.

In my last league, during a semi-final game, I tweaked my hamstring in the first minute of play. There I was, a 71-year-old man playing in an over-50 league. I nearly played the entire game. We were losing late when I stuck my hand into a passing lane. The ball was thrown so hard it broke my finger. Between that and the hamstring, I was convinced that my days in the league were over.

I was playing well at my level. I could have continued, but I started to worry about a serious injury. There is an over-55 league now and many of my friends still play. Those years were a wonderful part of my life. I made many good friends and was fortunate to have some of them become life insurance clients.

In 2014, I was honored by the Jewish Basketball League. Nelson Ralus nominated me. My family was at the banquet when I gave a 10-minute speech, which was well received. Bruce Drysdale, my old teammate from Lincoln, was in the audience. He took a picture with my sons, which still is hanging on a wall in our home.

It was nice to be recognized for the skills that made me a valuable member of the teams I played on. In 30 years, I played on 11 championship teams and lost nine times in the finals.

In the last championship game I won, I played most of the game without taking a shot. I could have, but I always passed to a teammate who had a better chance of making the shot. I did guard a top offensive forward on the other team and held him to three baskets. My teammates recognized my contribution, and that is all that mattered to me.

Playing in all of those championship series is something I am proud of to this day. The happiest moment, however, did not come from any of those championships or the ones I coached.

Telling Adam to pass the ball to his teammates in game two of their series was my best moment. They came back to win that game and the next and beat a heavily favored team. The boys were so excited and happy. For me, that was something truly special.

Sonny Hill Inspires Me

NAVIGATING THROUGH THE CHALLENGES OF LIFE can be difficult. For those with mentors, it becomes less arduous. In Philadelphia, we have a man named William "Sonny" Hill. Sonny grew up in North Philadelphia. He was born July 22, 1936, twenty years to the day after my mother. You may know him from watching *Basketball: A Love Story* on television.

Sonny loves baseball and especially basketball. He has a radio show every Sunday morning for two hours. He calls his spot "The Living Room." He invites callers to join in and talk about old-time basketball. He seems to know every basketball player of note in America. He has had many former basketball greats appear on his show. I have heard Earl "the Pearl" Monroe and Oscar Robertson speak on the show, among many other legends.

Sonny considers Wilt Chamberlain the greatest basketball player of all time. If you base your evaluation purely on overall skills, I would certainly agree with his assessment. However, there were two unexplained occurrences in my opinion that tarnish his reputation. In a game seven against the Celtics, he failed to take a single shot and the 76ers lost. Why? Not one shot? Unfathomable. In another championship game, he asked out of a game in the fourth quarter. William "Butch" Van Breda Koff was the coach. He was furious at Wilt. Bill Russell, who was announcing the game, questioned why Wilt went out. Russ said Chamberlain should not have come out, but his knee was seriously injured. Wilt and Bill, who were close friends prior to Bill's comment, became estranged for many years. Wilt won two NBA championships, and if he had the competitive demeanor of Michael Jordan or Larry Bird, he would have won at least two more.

For example, in the 1969 final Russell picked up five fouls, and Chamberlain should have called for the ball and attacked Russell every time down court. Without Russell, the Lakers might have won, because as great a defensive player as Russell was, and he was probably the greatest of all time, if Wilt was consistently aggressive Russell would never have been able to stop him.

Sonny Hill was a very fine basketball player at Northeast High School. He and his backcourt mate, Tee Parham, were formidable players. Tee and Sonny played many years in the Eastern Basketball League. What Sonny valued most were the people, like Guy Rodgers, who helped mentor him when he was growing up. As a result, he decided to give something back.

He started the Baker League one summer. Great players came from all over to play. Sonny gave opportunities to young men with ambition to play in college and professionally. I saw many of the games. The competition and the skill level of the players was exceedingly high. Sonny befriended many young men over the years. Most of them never made any money playing basketball, but they all became better people, and that was always Sonny's ultimate goal.

I've had the privilege of speaking on the phone and emailing with Sonny. He is a class guy and an asset to many of the youth of Philadelphia. He has inspired me to formulate my own vision for these kids.

There are many empty nesters in Philadelphia, and quite a few are retired and live in Center City. Their children are raising their own families, which means they have time and many of them possess the desire to give something back to their community. The skill levels they possess range from good to extraordinary. Some are musicians, artists, or teachers, writers, poets, or mechanics. They may play chess or have strong technical skills.

Many children, especially in the inner city, could benefit from their skills.

My concept is currently in the early stages, but here are its essential elements:

1. A matching system of 100 children with 100 adults.
2. Each adult involved in the program must submit a resume and list of physical and life skills they have to offer to their respective student.
3. Students must write what they are looking to achieve while participating in the program. Meetings twice a month on Saturday mornings for 90 minutes.
4. Venues in various neighborhoods throughout Philadelphia. Companies would donate some spaces, or we would use city or state property.
5. Children would be matched with mentors for writing or mechanics or possibly medical training.
6. The key element is to provide opportunities for people to help fellow people.
7. Program runs from September to June. At the end of each three-month period, the mentor and student would be required to write a written evaluation of each other. Honest critical dialogue is an essential part of the program.

Chills Down My Spine

I LOVE MUSIC LIKE I LOVE BASKETBALL. It's created a rhythm, literally and figuratively, in my life since I was a child and later as a teenager, driving around in the car, listening to all kinds of music on my AM radio.

Many years ago, when it came time to choose a location for the Rock and Roll Hall of Fame, the final contestants were boiled down to Philadelphia or Cleveland. One day, while standing on Market Street, west of City Hall, I watched a rally with speeches, urging the committee to vote for our city. I agreed that the city of Philadelphia, with its rich history of performers and the home of American Bandstand, was the natural choice.

I never understood why Cleveland was selected. Larry Magid, the music guru of Philadelphia, recently told me that political and financial considerations got in the way. That doesn't make much sense, because Philadelphia, located right off I-95, is in the middle of a much more heavily populated area on the east coast.

In my opinion, we didn't try hard enough. Had it been up to me, I would have pushed harder so that we got the venue, which would still be bringing in many visitors to help our local economy. As far as I know, the hall in Cleveland does not make money and is bailed out every year by their induction ceremony.

Some of the inductees, or those not selected, continue to puzzle me. For instance, why isn't Warren Zevon in there? What about Jerry

Butler? Why isn't Johnny Maestro of the Crests and the Brooklyn Bridge included?

Not long ago, while on my way to see Tony, my barber, on Market Street, I knocked on the window of an office two doors away where Jerry Blavet has been playing doo-wop music for more than 50 years. When I was a senior at the University of Pennsylvania back in 1962, I heard his show from a station in Camden, New Jersey. Jerry was white, but he loved playing music by black musicians. We had great black disc jockeys in Philadelphia. George Woods, "the man with the goods," was my favorite. He had a cow bell and loved to ring it. I loved "Story Untold" by the Nutmegs, and every time I heard him play it I got the chills, especially during the opening. Jock Henderson was the other great black disc jockey. They played black doo-wop, and I loved it. All the sponsors were black businesses.

WIBG consisted of all white DJ 's playing white pop music by mostly white singers. Pat Boone would sing black songs, but they were dreadful.

Jerry Blavet loved all of that music and he knew every group. He played the most obscure groups. On that day when I knocked on his window, he surprised me by coming outside to shake my hand and give me a copy of his book. I told him about this book and how I was planning to mention him with great affection.

"We'll have coffee someday," he said.

I will definitely push for that.

I listen to doo-wop every morning. Although I like every form of music, there is something special about doo-wop. The internet, especially Pandora and YouTube, have been a godsend for folks like me who love these old favorites. There have also been some great doo- wop concerts I have seen on WHYY fundraisers, with Jerry Butler, a Rock and Roll Hall of Famer, serving as the emcee.

Nowadays, instead of being limited to AM/FM radio, I listen to Sirius Radio in my car. I love listening to the special stations for specific artists, including Tom Petty, The Beatles, Bruce Springsteen and Billy Joel, who are among my favorites.

Meg Griffin is my favorite disc jockey. She really knows music and has a great, distinctive voice. Back in the day, she worked at the same station in New York City as Howard Stern. I used to listen to him every day back in the 80s and 90s. His honesty and ongoing rap were so appealing. Adam listens to him now and really likes him. He is especially appealing to guys, and I understand how some women could find him obnoxious. That's what's so good about radio today. The choices are endless!

Never Too Late

APPROXIMATELY TWO YEARS AGO, I presented an idea to Allan Domb, a well-known real estate magnate and political figure in Philadelphia. Years earlier, he confided, he had also been disappointed that our city had not been selected as the site for America's only Rock and Roll Hall of Fame. Both of us had been searching for some way to honor our city as a bedrock and bastion of great music, and I was excited to share my ideas with Allan.

I originally wanted to develop a Philadelphia Music Museum, which I later changed to The Philadelphia Music Experience, because the word "museum" can denote a sense of stodginess.

My plan included using an existing building or erecting a or new one, north of City Hall, as close to Broad Street as possible. It would have four floors and a usable basement. In the lobby would be a bandstand and a gift shop.

There would a permanent visual display of the Philadelphia area's great musicians from all genres of music. Gamble and Huff, Larry Magid, Jerry Blavet and Dick Clark would also be honored in our own local hall of fame. A steady stream of pianists would play all day, featuring music made famous by Philadelphians. In the basement we would feature a food court that would be distinctly Philadelphian, featuring cheese steaks, soft pretzels, pizza, hamburgers, sushi, healthy salads and locally grown vegetables.

Floor One would highlight classical artists, including Marion Anderson, Mario Lanza, and the Philadelphia Orchestra.

Music could be accessed by earphones and inside film rooms.

Floor Two would feature rock and roll, soul, doo-wop and gospel, with artists such as Bill Haley, Patti Labelle. Bobby Rydell, Frankie Avalon, Fabian, Lee Andrews, The Hearts, and all the dynamic artists who make up TSOP—The Sound of Philadelphia-- such as The Temptations, The Blue Jays, Three Degrees, and Harold Melvin and the Blue Notes.

Floor Three would include a section for jazz, showcasing John Coltrane, The Heath Brothers, and many more. There would also be a pop section for artists such as Eddie Fisher and Pink, and special sections devoted to rap, hip hop, and the blues.

A skilled musical curator could bring all this together, as I'm sure I've forgotten many artists and musical genres that are unique to the city of Philadelphia.

Finding a site north of City Hall on or near Broad Street would be the challenge, but it's certainly something that can be accomplished. There is an area near the Schuylkill River, between Market and Lombard, which would be a worthy site to consider.

When I spoke to Larry Magid, he had a succinct response.

"Find 100 million dollars and call me back. At that point, I'll be glad to assist with the project."

My attorney, Michael Shectman, drafted a proposal and sent it certified to David Cohen, an executive with Comcast. We outlined all the reasons why the venture would be profitable:

1. There would be founders with their names on a wall in the lobby, who would pay handsomely for this honor, as well as lifetime members and annual subscribers.

2. There would be a small $5 monthly charge for getting music and videos streamed to a subscriber's phone, radio or TV. For example, this would contain a doo-wop song and then possibly a classical piece, followed by a rap song. To the best of my

knowledge, there is no eclectic approach like this currently in existence.

3. There would be a clothing line for sale on site and on a dedicated website. They would all feature a G-clef insignia, which would be the branded visual of the enterprise.

4. There would be a room dedicated to hosting weddings, parties, and corporate functions. Hotels would sell packages including passes to the site.

Our city would reap significant revenue from hotel taxes, sales from food, and a variety of gift shops items, including valuable memorabilia. Parking would also bring in more revenue.

Veterans and people with significant disabilities would get in free. I would want an amateur night, where bands or individuals could compete for cash prizes.

The most important part would be creating a place where people would want to return again and again to see famous guests, new performers, and innovative music that normally has trouble finding a venue.

The potential revenue to the city would more than pay for the services they would need to provide, such as security, traffic supervision, and public notices.

A percentage of all revenue would provide scholarships for city high school graduates. Community college and vocational training costs would be awarded annually.

While Mr. Cohen at Comcast has not yet responded, we have reached out to Ed Rendell, asking him to intercede. So far, he has been too busy with other matters. I would like to approach potential prominent investors in the entertainment field with strong ties to Philadelphia. They include Bradley Cooper, Tina Fey, Kevin Bacon, Kobe Bryant, and Will Smith, among others.

I believe in my concept for The Philadelphia Music Experience. It would be a game changer for the city. The combination of culture, history and the music should be very appealing to tourists from all over the world. Everyone loves music of some kind, and they also love to eat. The menu for both should appeal to everyone's diverse tastes, so that we can create a great sense of community. That's what Philadelphia is all about!

RICHARD G. KRASSEN

To Live and Die with the Home Team

I HAVE BEEN A FAN OF THE PHILLIES since 1948, and last year hit rock bottom for me. The team was 64-49 and in first place in their division after 113 games. What an illusion. Real baseball fans knew the team had many problems.

The starting pitching was highly suspect. They should have added a left-handed starter in the off season. The manager, flushed with endless analytics, made highly questionable positional moves on the field. Hitters became clueless and struck out at an alarming rate. When the Phillies didn't hit home runs, they almost never won. Small ball was like a rotary phone, relegated to the dust heap of nostalgia. Hit and run was a foreign concept. No one could execute a bunt. We paid a huge amount of money for a free-agent starting pitcher who had a disinterested approach to almost every game he pitched and showed no real desire to win. Players were moving all over the field, and the batting order changed regularly.

Over the last 49 games, the Phillies played badly enough to almost make me wonder why I still rooted for them. Almost. God forbid I should ever become a fair-weather fan. No way.

Throughout the entire sickening slump, the manager repeatedly claimed that we had a terrific team, and swore by his players. I could picture him in 1912, realigning the deck chairs on the Titanic.

One thing he obviously did not know: In Philadelphia, if a team is playing badly, you say so. When players aren't performing, you try to improve their productivity, or you put in different players who get the job done.

Take for example, the 76ers. I stopped watching the 76ers early this year. They recently added Jimmy Butler to the team. I am interested again and have started watching. They play well at home. Most of the time, they don't play that way on the road. JJ Reddick is a great pro and I love watching him. The bench has some good players. They still need some more players to contend.

There are three major problems with this team, and I see no reason to be optimistic about them being corrected any time soon. The people involved have to take ownership and change the way they operate.

Ben Simmons is supremely talented. He has no shot besides a layup and a floater every now and then. He makes questionable decisions, especially against top teams, and he turns the ball over way too much. He needs to shoot 100 foul shots every day and make over 75 percent. He should also post up more than he does. No guard can stop him close to the basket, so why don't we see him doing that more?

All the triple double stats mean nothing to me, either. This man has the makings of a Hall of Fame candidate. He must dig deeper into himself and become much more productive on the court.

Joel Embiid is an outstanding talent, too, to say the least. He has serious flaws, however. He is soft and does not like or embrace physical contact. He should be fighting for position in the low block, not shooting three-point shots 25 feet from the basket where he's too far away to follow up his misses. Strong, physical centers, like they have on the Toronto Raptors, regularly outplay him. He has more talent and athleticism than they do and should take advantage of that.

The pick and roll is fine, but don't forget there will be no championships won without the proper mindset.

Jordon, Kobe, Bird, and Russell knew what was needed. Just watch old clips of them winning championships and you'll see exactly what I mean.

The 76ers have had several good coaches over the years. In 1983,

292

Billy Cunningham was the coach. He spent half his time screaming at Andrew Toney to play better defense.

Brett Brown has been the coach for many years. He is a fine man, passionate and badly wants to win. However, until he shows me he will get in the face of Embid and Simmons and get them to raise their games significantly, mark my words: there will be no championship in Philadelphia.

Baseball is like chess. It is a cerebral game. The battle between the pitcher and the hitter is more interesting to me than what I can appreciate about any other major sport. With the ball in his hand, the pitcher has the advantage. He attacks the hitter with a variety of pitches, speeds, and locations. Prior to the game, the batter has to study what pitches he will see in different situations. He should review how the pitcher has gotten him out before. The hitter should also know where he wants the ball to be before he swings. The hitter should concentrate on making good contact and using all fields. Pete Rose, Stan Musial, and Ichiro Suzuki were excellent examples of this type of hitting.

Strikeouts matter to me. I don't like them. Nowadays, I hear people talking about hitting the ball on a trajectory and avoiding ground balls. That is nonsense. Analytics may be valuable, but they are far from the only thing that matters when it comes to evaluating how a man hits a baseball.

When it comes to winning, analysis is good. The Phillies often struggle to analyze themselves correctly and make the proper changes required to become a serious contender. Their manager, general manager and owner all want to win. Understanding how to win, and what it takes, is quite another thing.

Succeeding in life means trying, failing, and making adjustments. What are the adjustments the Phillies are making? Making a big splash with a showy signing will not solve the problem. Maybe if they watch Ichiro's approach to hitting, they might get it.

The manager wants to learn and get better. I respect that. He can start by thinking for himself as to what might make his team better.

Unless the Phillies start playing like they are real contenders, our manager might be fired and gone.

But I will always be a Phillies fan.

A Win-Win for Philadelphia

ADAM WAS RECENTLY AT A SENIOR CENTER to speak about Medicare and the value of a supplemental insurance benefit. Adam is an expert in his field and has helped many appreciative people take good care of their situations.

One day, he met a man who had fought at The Battle of the Bulge and knew General Patton. My son thanked him for his service. Many people who made it back from wars of any kind consider themselves very fortunate. They still remember their fellow soldiers dying in front of their eyes, and many suffer from survivor's guilt.

I've been to two funerals recently for men who were younger than I when they passed. Both were highly regarded dentists with practices a mile from each other, and they died on the same day.

Harris Mann played basketball with me for many years and was also a steady client of mine. Maxine, his wife, was a corporate executive, dedicated wife, and mother to their two daughters.

Alan Frieman was Carole's dentist for all of her adult life. His wife, Marjorie Brody, is a very close friend of hers. I have known them since 1997. Alan loved golf; we enjoyed each other's company, even though I don't play.

When you are nearing 80 years old and have seen so many people pass away who were younger than you, it's time to count your blessings. My day is coming. I know that. I am trying to tie up loose ends before I can no longer do so.

In fact, I would like to use this book as a forum to put forth ideas that might help the people of Philadelphia, especially children growing up in the inner city, many of them without fathers or positive male role models. Even Philadelphia's public schools are short on male teachers, especially African-American men.

Several neighborhoods in my beloved city are struggling mightily because so many of their boys and men have been arrested and sent to prison, often for petty crimes or no crime at all. There are bright black men in prisons who work hard and get degrees online and can become teachers.

Why don't some of them get hired by the city? People in prison deserve an opportunity. It would be good for everyone, a win-win all around—socially, economically, and otherwise—if we could reform this system. Philadelphia could even become a model for the rest of the country.

Change like this requires a team effort.

In basketball and in all major sports, teams go on runs. When that happens, everything is working, and the team wins most every game. In my senior year of high school, we won 14 straight games. Most games were close, but we found a way to win. Teamwork, hard work, and persistence were the keys to our success.

The United States of America has been on a run. Since surviving the war with England, we have been blessed with ongoing success and relative prosperity, at least for the majority of our citizens. We have wonderful natural resources. We have secure borders. We have been in wars, but despite the dubious choice of becoming involved in the first place, we have managed to keep ourselves at peace here at home. We finally recognized that slavery was wrong, but unfortunately racism is still alive and well throughout our society.

The core of our problem is simple. America has been taken over by greed. I thoroughly believe in capitalism, but it has its share of faults. For example, when quarterly profits are magnified to the point of ignoring our collapsing infrastructure and the negative effects of climate change, we have a problem.

I have an idea that should be studied.

Many people are in prisons today all across the country for making a mistake. Some of them have been egregious, but many are not. The cost to our nation's budget for housing, feeding and "rehabilitating" them has become staggering. Prisons have become a big business. This has to stop. These people can be trained to build our nation's infrastructure. They need an opportunity to gain a feeling of self-worth and could also work off their sentences for their own benefit and for that of our country.

Successful work records should reduce time served. Once these men and women are out of prison, they will have viable skills to continue working in the construction industry. It is a win-win situation, and I'd like to see my own city and state lead the way in making this type of reform happen.

Meeting My Childhood Idols

BEFORE ROBIN ROBERTS BECAME a great pitcher for the Phillies, he was a terrific basketball player at Michigan State University. I tried to listen to every inning he pitched. When he lost, I was inconsolable. He was a great competitor and I was his biggest fan.

In the spring of 2009, I got a phone call from my good friend, Allan Marmon, who lived in a senior community in Bucks County, inviting me to a luncheon there that Robin Roberts would be attending. I was beyond excited. I was going to meet my boyhood idol! What could be better than that? When I arrived, Irwin Pearlstein, an old basketball buddy, was there and gave me a baseball for Robin to sign.

I met Robin and shook his hand. He was 83 years old and seemed very physically fit. We spoke briefly, and he signed my ball, "To Rich, a great fan."

It got even better. After lunch, people asked him questions. I raised my hand and mentioned one of his toughest defeats in 1952, when Whitey Lockman hit a 279-foot opposite field homer to beat him and the Phils one to nothing. I told him about games he pitched, recounting each batter he faced and what they did at bat. He looked at me in absolute awe. He remembered every at bat, too.

I recited all of that to show my boyhood idol how much he meant to me, and to have him take it in was a genuine highlight of my life.

Robbie died the following year at age 84.

I hope that moment when we connected was as important to him as it was for me.

By now, you know how important basketball has been to me throughout my life. I grew up idolizing a player named Tom Gola, one of the classiest players to ever play the game. His fundamentals were unmatched. He could do everything and play every position.

I never met him, but I saw him play several times. His LaSalle team won the NCAA championship in 1954. Frank Blatcher played on that team. He came off the bench and scored 23 points to beat Bradley. I met Frank at a basketball dinner once, and he told me his life story.

Tom passed away in 2014. I attended the funeral service in a church in Huntingdon Valley. I told his wife that I had never met her husband, but I was there to pay my respects to someone I always admired, on and off the court.

My Love of Puns

WHEN MY CHILDREN WERE TEENAGERS, we considered a trip to Tuscan, Arizona. We were ready to go when I realized it was a bad idea. I would have to leave one of my three boys at home.

I read obituaries in the newspapers every day. I want to see if any of my old friends or clients have died. When people die, they mention their "late" husbands or wives. I came to realize the importance of punctuality.

I read about three young Wall Street guys from North Jersey. They had fancy cars and drove into New York City every weekday morning. They met for lunch one day and decided they would take turns going in every day together since they lived a short distance from each other. They listened to sports and swapped stories and had a good time. After about a year, they all began experiencing pain up and down their wrist and forearm. They went to see a specialist. The diagnosis was "carpool tunnel syndrome."

Adam has a girlfriend, Susan, who works for a travel agency. She is planning a trip to Vietnam and has continually urged him to go with her. In a moment of pith, he told me he has started to find the whole thing very "Hanoi-ing."

Like father, like son. We both love puns.

Why stop here? Here are a few more, just for fun:

A friend of mine had to have a hip replacement. He was required by law to sign a HIPPA form. If he needed a knee replacement, is he required to sign a KNEE form?

I once met a young man in Washington Square Park. He looked worried, so I asked him if he was okay. He said he just asked his girlfriend to marry him and she said yes.

"We promised each other complete transparency," he said. "She told me her mother was an alcoholic and her father was arrested years ago for tax fraud."

"Were you okay with that?" I said.

He nodded.

"I told her one brother was in jail for selling drugs and the other was listed as a pedophile."

"Was she okay with that?" I said.

"Yeah, she was fine."

"So, what is wrong?"

"I didn't her about my third brother."

Oh my God, what's his problem?

"He's a life Insurance salesman."

My wife and I went to the Philadelphia Museum of Art on a cold day. We checked our coats and there was no charge. The sign said, "complementary coat check." Before we left the museum, we retrieved our coats, and I took note of the sign.

"You have a beautiful smile," I said to the young woman.

Lessons Learned

AS ONE GROWS OLDER, you learn that it's not love that makes the world go 'round. It's money. We all have to survive. Animals know their enemies. They learn that shortly after birth. Humans, with their advantages and disadvantages, learn this somewhat differently. People can reason and think, and those who are lucky, by birth or through other means, have a lot more choices in their everyday life.

The problem is, enemies are all around us and we don't often realize it. Parents care for their babies and children but are not always keenly aware of what lessons are best to teach their offspring. As a result, many parents do not adequately prepare their children for the real world. Consequently, children grow up with friends and sleepovers and birthday presents. The value of money and what it takes to earn it is rarely discussed. I grew up and enjoyed my childhood, but I never really understood the deadly game that life can often be.

Every child becomes his or her own corporation and CEO. Every decision is important. Acquiring skills and knowledge elicit feelings of self-confidence, which is a delicate thing to maintain in the right form. One screw-up with your kids, your wife, your boss, your parents, your friends, or your siblings can change everything. We are all packages. Some things about us are to be admired and some things are more appropriately scoffed at.

The problem with formal education is that much of what is being taught is a collection of rote subjects and facts based on the past. Teachers who are genuinely valuable make their students think critically *now* and consider finding solutions for what they will face in the future.

Once upon a time, Eastman Kodak was a fine, blue-chip company. As more and more new products came onto the market, they did not continue to evolve and eventually became less valued and almost irrelevant. Sadly, they were not the only company who fell asleep at the wheel of progress.

The future is all that really matters to any of us. Winning the Super Bowl last year was a treasured memory for any dedicated fan of the Eagles. This is a new year, however, which also means this team has to prove itself all over again, which so far it is not.

The greatest attribute capitalism possesses is that through an incentive to earn profits, new products are produced, and their cost is constantly evaluated so that these products can be produced at the lowest fixed costs possible. According to that theory, industries and services continue to change, and some are eliminated if they do not meet current standards.

The coal industry should be a good example. In some areas, it has disappeared, to be replaced by safer and greener means of creating energy for consumption. Unfortunately, the industry lives on and is even being expanded in some cases because of old-fashioned values and simple greed.

As individuals, we can only do so much to move the needle. For each of us, the key to surviving is staying ahead of the curve.

Parents in many parts of the world are obsessed with their child's academic success. Getting into the right school and finding a secure place in society is the goal. Teaching children the value of academic success and achievement is a good thing.

When children grow up, their ability to make a good living is paramount. Going to the best school isn't mandatory. Doing a job you feel passionate about is more important. Making a living while feeding your passion is a blessing. I was a zombie until I was 40. I felt no passion, except for sports and music. I couldn't make a steady living doing either. Fortunately, I found my passion and became moderately successful at selling life insurance. I got my first license in 1963. Fifty-five years later, I am still at it. My wife asks me why I'm still doing this. It is in my DNA. This is what I do.

The friends I was fortunate enough to make saved my life. Many bought life insurance policies from me or referred me to business associates, friends or family members.

There are harsh lessons to be learned from what I experienced:

1. Associate with people who have empathy.
2. Help people and compliment them whenever possible.
3. Value your time and make it work for you.
4. Be selfish about your own needs.
5. Find your passion and believe in it.
6. Evaluate your strengths and weaknesses and find people who will complement your weaknesses with their strengths.

Life is complex. There are plenty of experts and companies that will prey on your negative feelings about yourself with ads for products dealing with issues such as erectile dysfunction, hair loss, or high cholesterol.

Find alternatives to all the temptations. Try things that don't cost money, like hiking, biking, reading, or listening to music—my favorites.

Proud Grandpa

ELI AND MILES LOVE TO PLAY BASKETBALL. They share that love with me. They both play in community leagues, and Eli, who is 6'1" already at age 14, also plays travel ball. Charlie, my step-grandson in Venice, California, is a fine baseball player. He pitches and plays shortstop. I watch him play when Carole and I visit.

All three grandsons play the piano. Eli and Miles play instruments, too.

My three granddaughters are doing well. Sydney, the oldest, graduated from the University of Wisconsin and now works for a non-profit in New York City. Blair is a junior at University of the Arts in Philadelphia. She hopes to be a playwright. Erin lives in Northridge, California. She shows promise as an artist and is taking violin lessons. Her Aunt Sharon and Carole are both fine artists.

I'm Not Running for Office, But If I Were . . .

BY THE TIME YOU REACH THE WORLD of senior citizenship, you have been around the block at least a few times and should have learned quite a bit. It also means you have formed a collection of strong opinions and don't have a lot of time to suffer too many fools, or much interest in putting up with too much nonsense.

That said, it's never too late to get smarter and take better care of yourself. Several years ago, after my doctor told me I was a prediabetic, I began to diet and exercise. I went from 209 pounds to 185. My A1C is about normal now. I thank my doc for that.

My last doctor, however, wanted me to go on cholesterol medicine. I decided to fire that doctor and find a new one. My new doctor does not think I need cholesterol medicine. That's fine with me, because I do not want to be on a list looking for a liver in ten years. At that age, there will be no list for me. It's sad. Too many doctors opt for the easy fix with pills. Since the pharmaceutical lobby is so intense, many unfortunate people end up talking medicine they may not need. For the ones that do need it, they often end up paying a high cost, which could eat up all their savings. In some cases, they suffer endless side effects, too.

The pharmaceutical industry hires many people to do their bidding, and this industry seems to be ridiculously profitable. But is it equitable and responsible for everyone it serves? I don't think so. Poor and middle-income people suffer greatly if they have a medical condition that requires expensive medicine. I don't know how this can be fixed, but our lawmakers better do something before it gets totally out of hand, even more than it is now.

That brings me to a few thoughts on our politics today.

Our current campaign finance rules allow for unlimited spending, which means that large corporations have tremendous leverage about many reforms. I think there should be cap limits with an adjustable increase for inflation. It's the only way to keep a level playing field. Big money buys big favors. That affects global warming, the cost of drugs, and the unfettered manufacturing and sale of high-powered assault weapons.

The argument for the Second Amendment allowing gun ownership is fine. It is part of our country's heritage. Most gun owners are responsible. I get it. So why doesn't the NRA do everything in its power to keep unhealthy people from obtaining dangerous weapons?

No one is coming for anyone's guns, as they claim. That is a scare tactic. Arming teachers is a bad idea, too. Having a healthy citizen network to report to a 24-hour-a-day, anonymous tip line about possible potential terrorist acts is one answer. This should include reporting family members, too. A task force like this would follow up and have the ability to take guns away from those who should not have them. Companies who sell guns and market them also have a responsibility to the greater good of society.

Preventing acts of violence is our only hope. Living in a more peaceful environment will help us focus on other problems we have not addressed, such as infrastructure and climate change. These should be our priorities, but the next quarterly profit report seems to be all that matters for those in charge. They build houses in bad areas, kill animals, and destroy the environment, all in the name of helping companies make more money. There is a delicate balance between helping companies expand and make profits while protecting our environment. Is it really that hard?

We should all be striving for the common good of our country and our planet. This is not about conservatives being right or liberals being wrong, or vice versa. Conservatives concerned about the deficit and making sure our military is cutting edge are right. They are also correct about our need for new immigration laws and that many of our existing social programs are ineffective and expensive. However, the deficit is growing right now under a Republican president. Separating mothers from their children at the border is wrong. Poor people are not lazy. That is a myth perpetuated against people of color.

Everyone in the world has an opinion on our president. Adam likes him, but Josh does not. I'm not sure about Paul.

I must say, Trump has charisma. He is a great pitchman, a tireless promoter for himself and other Republican hopefuls. He has shown himself to be brilliant at presenting himself as a man who wants to make America great again, whatever that means. His message has tapped into all the people in the country who have felt betrayed by former presidents. He makes other people the reason why the country is failing and has managed to attract about a third of the country who believe in him.

Hillary Clinton lost the election by ignoring the people that she needed to win. It was not Russia. It was her. She lost, and to this day she still refuses to see that or understand how it all worked. There were six states that mattered, and she had nothing for the rural people in those areas.

In my opinion, the Electoral College is fine. The way he played it, Trump deserved to win. He is a big personality and draws certain types of people to him. He knows his base. He will do whatever it takes to win. I admire that to a point. In his own way, he would like to support the best interests of our country, but his ego keeps getting in the way.

We are now all fearful of illegal immigration. There are people who apply and must wait their turn. That said, you don't rip children from their mothers to prove a point. That is barbaric.

The stock market is up since Trump took office, but the tax cut has sent the deficit soaring. Trump has no history of managing costs and there is no reason to believe he will start now.

His claim that he is a self-made man is a lie. He said he would bring back clean coal, which was another lie. I could go on with his lies, but then this book would get way too long.

Life is a team sport. We want every country, including ours, to be successful. When people and countries maintain their dignity and self-worth, wars can be prevented.

We compete with other countries for the betterment of all parties. China steals our intellectual property. The question is, what can we do to correct this practice? Skilled diplomacy is a better answer than all of our tariff warfare. We must use leverage and be tenacious, but while doing so we cannot hurt some of our own domestic companies.

The presidency is the hardest job in the world. It requires delegating jobs to brilliant people who want to serve the country. Trump has tremendous energy and he always thinks he is the smartest person in the room. That is a dangerous position because underestimating the people you are dealing with can produce unexpected and costly results.

The ruler of North Korea has an agenda. Unfortunately, dismantling existing missiles is not one of them.

In order for the Democrats to take back the White House they will need someone who can put forth a winning agenda and stand up to the President if he is once again the Republican candidate.

Every human being wants a sense of dignity. Everyone deserves respect. Many poor people stay poor because they are exploited. Michael Jordon, LeBron James, and many other high-profile black athletes sign shoe deals that quickly bring them lucrative financial gain. Poor kids buy these sneakers. The cost of these shoes as a percentage of family income is substantial. Kids should never buy those shoes. Kobe and LeBron and Michael are using those children to get rich. I get mad when I think of all those poor, inner-city kids paying $125 for a $10 pair of sneakers.

Most companies will do anything to sell you something you

don't need. They use Madison Avenue to convince you to spend more and more money every day. According to advertisers, maxing your credit card is okay. Running up large college debt is okay. Getting gouged for drugs is okay. Taking expensive, unaffordable trips is okay.

Professional people get paid loads of money in order to persuade consumers to spend *endless* amounts of money. These consumers are rarely conscious that they are paying hard-earned, after-tax dollars on every purchase.

I've learned to save money on the basics. I never go to Starbucks. I use a coffee maker at home. There are many ways people fall victim to spending money for something cute, like a special kind of coffee. It is all marketing and bullshit. Make purchases that make sense.

The soda industry is another pet peeve of mine. I haven't had a soda in more than three years. It is unhealthy and expensive.

Spend your money wisely. You worked hard for it.

This brings me to the subject of student college debt and the burden it creates for students and families.

A college sells itself because of its campus and all the bells and whistles it can present to get a student to enroll.

"Come now and pay later."

It's absurd that an undergraduate education in the United States costs so much. Colleges are in the education *business* and what courses you take and what you major in is really of no concern to them. When a student graduates with a debt of $100,000 and can't get a job to pay it back, it means nothing to them. When it comes to the universities running things and making money, you are not a repeat customer. They don't care. On the other hand, a restaurant needs you to come back in order to stay in business.

This approach seems to be working. So when a student goes to college, he or she should be asking some key questions and then make a business decision. For example, how is that college going to provide me what I need to make money? Excuse me, but the parents should make the choice, not an 18-year-old child.

I read a sad story about a young woman who had the chance to go to college for free. Instead, she chose to go to the school of her choice, which costs $280,000. Her parents went along with her wishes. If she were my daughter, she would have gone where it was free, assuming the school offered a decent education.

It should not be a parent's goal to have their child like them. If your financially responsible choice is upsetting for them, too bad. I told Josh he had to go to Ursinus College for pre-med because there was no choice. The school was under the radar, but very well priced at the time. It offered a good education at a fair price. He graduated and went to The School of Osteopathic Medicine. He is now a physiatrist and lives a nice life.

Parents must learn about the various scholarships, which are available nationwide. In 10th grade, parents should find out their options and the child should do what is necessary to qualify.

Universities are money guzzlers. They should allow students to attend partly in person and partly online. That would keep costs down while not sacrificing the quality of education. There is no reason for costs to exceed $15,000 to $20,000 a year. There should be work available to help offset the cost. Drexel always has work programs available for upper classmen. All colleges should have them. There should also be alumni lists available to graduating students to help them get placed in a job. The pervasive thinking today, that if you don't go to college your future earnings will be less than those having a high school diploma, is nonsense. That data is flawed because there are plenty of high school graduates who learn a trade and become successful. Some people graduate college and have little chance of finding a good job that pays well.

The burden of being a student remains an albatross around the neck of many graduates. They have no credit and can't buy a home or an automobile. How can they start a family?

Colleges and universities are living a charmed life. They are non-profit institutions, which is ridiculous. They should be taxed because they are a money-making *business*. The University of Pennsylvania is run to be a successful business. At a certain point, there should be a cap on assets. These schools should be forced to lower tuition costs and fees and give more scholarships, or else they should face severe tax consequences.

We muddle along with the same ol', same ol'. We need student awareness programs and high school guidance counselors who are better trained so that every graduating student has a chance to get an education without building up insurmountable debts.

Life is a battle to survive, and kids should get a chance to enter adulthood without a financial mountain to climb.

That's the end of my rant, for now.

I am trying to live out the rest of my life as meaningfully as I can. I appreciate everyone who has taken time out of their busy lives to read my life story. Thank you.

We are all in this together. Let's be good to each other.

Enjoying the Italian Market in Philadelphia.
(Photo courtesy of Linda Resnick)

Carole and I on our wedding day, 2004.

At wedding, (left to right) stepson, Alex, Paul, me, Josh and Adam.

Granddaughters Blair and Sydney at our 2004 wedding.

Carole and her twin daughters, Sharon (left) and Deborah (right),
along with Erin, Deborah's daughter (2018).

Original art by Carole.

My sister, Ellen.

Paul, playing his first love.

Adam, high school basketball referee.

*Two grandsons (middle) playing against each other
in community basketball league, and at home with Josh and me.*

Miles, Eli, Paul and me, enjoying a night out.

Eli, my grandson, and I, on the Klein Branch court.

My granddaughter, Erin, with her artwork.

My grandson, Charlie, with his Good Sportsmanship award.

Tom Carey, friend and author,
At our 60th high school reunion, 2018.

Ed Biasi, a schoolmate, at our 60th high school reunion, 2018.

*Ernie Beck, former University of Pennsylvania All-American
basketball player and Philadelphia Warrior in the NBA.*

My long-time basketball friend, Ace,
a former Philadelphia fireman.

A treasured baseball autographed by Robin Roberts.

Wali Jones (left) and Ken Hamilton.

Carole (my muse and beloved wife) and I, at Vedge restaurant, celebrating the 21st anniversary of our first meeting.

Celebrating our 14th anniversary
at Friday, Saturday, Sunday restaurant.

Josh and I at the Eagles victory parade, February 2018.

A favorite mural of mine at Broad and Tasker,
featuring Jerry Blavat, Chubby Checker, Bobby Rydell
and many more Philadelphia music icons.
(Photo courtesy of Linda Resnick)

AFTERWORD

Leaving a Legacy

SUSAN PASSED AWAY RECENTLY. She was a vital part of my life story, since we lived together for more than 30 years. Our three sons and four grandchildren would not exist without her. Susan's passing has been upsetting to all of us.

This past summer, I embarked on a special project with my grandsons, Miles and his brother, Eli. On a rainy day in August, I headed out on the Schuylkill Expressway, going north from Center City. The outer lane had so much water that I was forced out of it and almost turned back. By the time I arrived to pick them up, the rain had subsided, and we headed back out to visit the old neighborhoods where I lived as a child, teenager, and young adult.

Our first stop was Temple Shalom at Roosevelt Boulevard and Large Street, where I celebrated my Bar Mitzvah and my first wedding, as well. The synagogue is now a church. There are few Jews still living in Oxford Circle. Miles used his camera to take photos.

Then we drove to 6704 Large Street, where I lived from age 13 to 23. It is a beautiful block, unlike any other in Oxford Circle, with large trees providing shade for the entire street of brick and stone, semi-detached homes.

I hoped to introduce myself to the owners, who had a security camera. Eli saw the blinds open, but the people were afraid to open the door. Maybe an old Jewish guy with white hair and two teenage boys looked like trouble, and I guess I can't blame them.

We then drove around the corner to 6749 Kindred, a row home where I lived from age two to 12. Miles took a picture of the steps where I used to play stepball. The wires at Knorr and Kindred were still there. Buried in the memory of those wires was my classic wireball game with Joe Silver.

Back in the car, we drove to the corner of Horrocks and Knorr streets, the perfect four corners where we once played boxball, a real scientific game and my favorite. We drove south on Horrocks until we arrived at Spruce Elementary School, where I was a student in 5th and 6th grades.

I started playing basketball in the playground of that school. I remember graduation day. We sang the songs of all the big colleges in Pennsylvania: Penn, Temple, and the University of Pittsburgh, among others.

We continued, driving to Solis Cohen, where I attended school in third and fourth grades. When we got hungry, we had lunch at the Country Club Diner, which opened around 1953. The place was remodeled, and the menu did not include the original Jewish foods sold back in the day. It was fine. We took a picture.

Across the street, on the opposite side of Cottman, stands Woodrow Wilson Middle School, which housed me from seventh to ninth grade. This was the home of my basketball success and the American Legion Award I received for doing my homework, which I actually did during that time.

We drove over to Ashbourne Road in Cheltenham, the home Carole and I lived in from 2000 to 2015. Miles took a few pictures. Then we continued to Greycourt Road in the Pine Valley neighborhood of Philadelphia. My first wife, Susan, and I lived there from 1966 to 1969. Josh and Adam were born during that time. The current residents were home, so we spoke to them about the history of the house, which was built by a builder named Bronstein in the early 1960s. We took a picture in front of two beautiful blue spruce trees, which I had originally helped to plant. They had grown magnificently.

Back in the car, we drove to the Klein Branch, where I played in basketball leagues for 30 years. We met Ace, a retired fireman and old friend. We played basketball together and went to a few Phillies games together.

Our last stop was at my old home in Huntingdon Valley, where I lived from 1970 until 1995. I raised my three sons there, in that nice suburban neighborhood with good schools and nice people.

The boys had a good time that day and so did I. Hopefully, they will remember me long after I'm gone. I'm doing all I can to ensure that my demise is still far down the road. I walk more than two miles every day and try to eat as healthily as possible. I love French fries and desserts and still eat them on occasion, but since every day is valuable, I do what I can to stay healthy.

It has been a wonderful journey so far. As far as I'm concerned, there is no better place to live than right here in Philadelphia. There is no place on earth I would rather live than at the St. JAMES Apartments in center city Philadelphia. I have a beautiful, eastern exposure, floor-to-ceiling view of Washington Park and the Delaware River.

I walk two to three miles every day. I speak to people in my building on the elevator. There are 45 floors and over 300 apartments. The building is pet friendly, with many dogs. They love it here. Carole and I walk everywhere. The buses for seniors are free. We rarely drive anywhere, which is fine by me. There are many good restaurants in the area, and entertainment options, too.

For me, it is like being on vacation every day. I love talking to strangers, even on bus rides, where I have short conversations. I love meeting people, many who don't look like me.

I am not a shore person. Every summer, we are invited by my brother-in-law, Robbie Levin, and his wife Suzanne, to spend a few days at their beautiful home in Harvey Cedars on Long Beach Island. I have visited Florida in the winter and although the weather is less challenging there, I am happy to spend my winters in Philadelphia. I have the proper clothing, which is 90 percent of what it takes to manage the cold and snow. There are a few tough days when the ice gets bad, but shoveling snow is no longer a problem. In the winter, I focus on all the exciting things to do and the cold becomes incidental.

I know many people who like the suburban life or the countryside, or Florida or other shore locations. I respect all of their preferences, but I have mine, and they are in Philly. I hope I have a few more healthy years to enjoy my surroundings right here.

We all have our flaws, of course, so the only thing we can do is try to be better—for our family, friends, and for whichever city it is that we love.

I have been asked why anyone will read this book. I've been reminded on more than one occasion that I am no one famous or special. The famous part is for sure, but I like to think that every now and then I qualify as special, as we all do.

With that in mind, I am writing this for all those who are not famous, which is most of us. We get up every morning and do the best we can with our decisions and our judgements. Sometimes we are wrong, and we pay the price. We get divorced or lose a job or face mental challenges, such as depression and anxiety. I check all the boxes, like many of us.

I also know I will probably get sick someday, and I when I die, I will be forgotten by most everyone. That's just a fact. Maybe one day one of my great-grandchildren will pick up the book and learn something new about a man they heard of, a city they are curious about, and a whole lot more. If family members pass my book down to each new generation, that will be good enough for me.

Thanks to each and every one of you who followed my breadcrumbs. I hope the journey has been worthwhile.

My Wish

Faded dreams at break of dawn,
A new year about to spawn,
A sincere wish for humanity's crew,
I hope life will be good to you.

ACKNOWLEDGMENTS

I WOULD LIKE TO THANK all the people who have played a role in my life. Many of you influenced me in ways you may not even be aware of, but I want to thank you all for your presence in my life at one time or another.

Specifically, I would like to acknowledge all of my clients who have purchased life insurance from me. I hope they like me a little more now than they did before.

My basketball coaches, Phil Golden and Harry Silcox, taught me much more than basketball, and I will always be grateful to them for that.

Norty Levine, a local basketball icon, was an inspiration for me. Thanks, too, to my basketball buddies at the Klein branch Y.

Tom Petty, I must acknowledge you. I've always loved you and your music. You died too soon. Hope to see you someday.

Linda Resnick did a great job contributing her original photographs and I appreciate her perspective on the city I love.

I'd like to thank David Tabatsky for helping me make this book a reality.

Of course I want to thank my parents Vera and Morris, who gave me life.

To my wife, Carole, my biggest fan and biggest critic, this book is dedicated to you, as am I.

Finally, let me send love to my children, Josh, Adam, and Paul, three precious jewels who have always made me proud.

One's family, those gone and those still here, are the people whose love and support contribute to your well-being. If not for them, and those I've always considered extended family, I wouldn't have written this book.

Thank you, one last time, for all you've given me and for all I've been able to share with you.

ABOUT the AUTHOR

Richard G. Krassen was born and raised in Philadelphia and still lives there today.

"This book is for all my fellow Philadelphians who may not be famous like me (still dreaming) but get up every morning and work hard for the people they love and will walk through fire if it would help their professional sports teams win, especially the Eagles. God bless all of you."

Washington Square Park, Philadelphia, 2018.
(Photo courtesy of Linda Resnick)

A portion of the proceeds from sales of this book will be donated to the *Make a Wish Foundation.*